Stretch-mark MY HEART

Building Our
Family through
Adoption One
Child (or Two)
at a Time

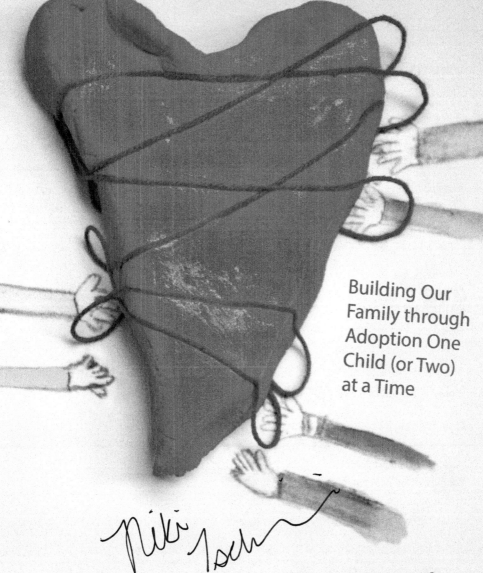

Niki Tsch

Niki Breeser Tschirgi

This book is a memoir and reflects my present remembrances of experiences over many years. I have changed some individual characteristics to maintain anonymity of the people involved. I have also tried to re-create events and conversations to the best of my recollection, making sure the heart of the story is not lost. I have done my very best to be truthful.

First published by Dog Ear Publishing
4011 Vincennes Rd
Indianapolis, IN 46268
www.dogearpublishing.net

ISBN: 978-1-4575-6215-0

This book is printed on acid-free paper.

Printed in the United States of America

Cover Illustration Copyright © 2018 by Tommy Tschirgi and Kelly Richards
Cover design by Carrie L. Case Creative
Book design and production by Dog Ear Publishing
Editing by Dog Ear Publishing
Author photograph by Heidi Pratt

To my husband, for without him,

we would not be the family that we are today.

Matt and Alex.

Acknowledgments

Thank You, God. Thank You for being present *always*. This journey has You so tightly woven through it, I couldn't possibly separate You from the details.

For Matt, my husband, who read and reread this book with enthusiasm, support, and unwavering belief that this story was meant to be shared.

For my children: Liza Ann Marie, Luis Joshua Isaac, Carlosse Richard Patrick, Alexander Steven Walter, Tommy Matthew Lyle, and Zackary Nicholas Calvin. You are my everything. You are my starfish.

Thank you, family, for loving us, for loving being a part of adoption: Grandma Mooshie, Uncle Cid, Auntie Tammy, Abby, Elli, Hallie, Grandma Anita, Grandpa Rich, Grandma Sheela, Uncle Scott, Auntie Susie, Samantha, Uncle Mike, Uncle Julien, Auntie Natalie, Hadrien, and Luke. For our extended family in Iowa and Wisconsin who have doted on our kids, especially their Auntie Ellen and Uncle Red Stick. Our children have so many more people to love them because of you.

Thank you, social workers and CASA workers: Hadiyah Conaté, an angel walking this earth, and Virginia Bond for volunteering her time, money, and fantastic efforts to keep siblings connected. Thank you, Shamara Moore, for your patient perseverance in helping us finalize Liza, Luis, Tommy, and Zack's adoptions while we lived in Dallas. Thank you, Joan Rhoades and Heather Lannigan, for your determined efforts to assist the children in and around the Pullman, Washington, area.

Special thanks to Adoption Services of Spokane (formerly Spokane Consultants), Depelchin Children's Center, Hope Cottage, and the great states of Washington and Texas. We are a direct reflection of your tireless efforts to place children with forever families.

To *all* of you who helped me with my book just because you love me: Gina Young, Dacia From, Carrie Case, Karin Grinzel, Matt Tschirgi, and Barb Breeser for pre-reading and editing. Thank you, Carrie Case, for your exceptional graphic design work, and Kelly Richards for your patient guidance with Tommy as he created my book cover. Thank you, Marsha Breeser, for reading almost every stage of the rough draft; *that* is being a true mom and champion!

Thank you, Denise Kendrick, for the beautiful call to action at the end of this book. Everyone can do something for kids in foster care.

Thank you, foster parents and adoptive families. Thank you for receiving children into your home. For loving them. For keeping them forever, and for letting them go. For making a difference. For your sacrifice of time, energy, sanity, and health. For the late nights nobody but God and your kids see. For the doctor appointments, school projects, late-night feedings, breakfasts, lunches, dinners, snacks, laughter, tears, heartbreak, and victory. For bike riding, school concerts, first steps, potty training, diaper changing, storytime, bedtime drama, meltdowns, and teenage angst. For praying, stressing, loving, cringing, advocating, collapsing, speaking, fuming, and simply being there. For counseling sessions, therapy sessions, family meetings, continuing education, and trainings. For cuddling, saying "I'm sorry" and "I love you," and sometimes just letting things be. Thank you for saying yes. Thank you for answering the call.

Contents

Foreword vii

Introduction: A Note from Niki 1

Preface: Twinkle, Twinkle Little Starfish 5

1. Infertility..7

2. Alex 15

3. Open Adoption...18

4. Little Brown Eyes...22

5. Big Brown Eyes..26

6. Carlosse 34

7. Foster Care 38

8. The Third Bedroom......................................46

9. Zack...53

10. There's Your Sign 58

11. Tommy..68

12. Summertime Sojourns 76

13. Liza and Luis..79

14. First Visit 84

15. Second Visit..86

16. A Mother's Right 90

17. Congratulations…It's Teenagers! 99

Afterword: A Call to Action................................103

Notes..107

Foreword

Stretch-mark My Heart contains the story of our adoption journey. We chose to create our family through adoption, meaning it was built from other families that had been broken apart. Most people looking in from the outside at our story may think it began with infertility, but for me, it started before that. Although most young men think about their favorite sports team, player, or career goals, I pondered my future children, even before marriage. I always had what I was told was an unfounded fear of not being able to have biological children. It didn't grip me but was always simmering in my periphery. This was not a rational thought and there was no evidence to support it, yet it was still there.

Infertility has been known to destroy even the strongest of marriages. Thankfully, it brought Niki and I closer together. There was a time in our relationship when we were navigating infertility, trying to decide how to cope, how to move forward, seeking God's plan, all the while building a firm foundation in our marriage. Has our marriage been challenged? Yes, but I believe our infertility experience has helped us weather some especially hard times as a couple and as parents. I believe infertility has made me more resilient because of my response, meaning I didn't wallow in our diagnosis. Adoption was a series of choices—some little, others big. It wasn't easy, but, looking back, I'm so glad we plotted the course we did.

I work in the field of genetics. I specialize in the study and diagnosis of heritable disease. How ironic is it that I have no biological children who share my DNA? I've been told most men have a strong desire to pass their genes to the next generation, which is why many in my situation choose medical intervention over adoption. I'm not saying this is wrong for others. It just wasn't right for us, or our six children.

Much of life consists of a series of crossroads—choices we make daily. While some are as trivial as what to have for breakfast or what television show to binge-watch, our choices may affect ourselves and others for eternity. The gravity of our choices and circumstances may not be apparent until we are on the other side, so to speak. Looking back to the sibling group of four we adopted, we see a combination of unique circumstances and choices that directed us to our children. At the time, some of those choices seemed inconsequential, but the fate of four of our children hung in the balance.

I hope Niki's rendering of our adoption story will warm your heart, make you laugh, and inspire you to go beyond yourself. As you will see, I have not been a spectator or tagalong through this process but an active partner with Niki. Each time we have said "yes" to adopt a child, we have made a conscious, unified decision. When I was a young man, never in a million years did I think I would adopt six children. It has stretched me beyond what I thought I could handle and has left marks on my heart, which is a good thing. I recognize that not everyone is called to adopt even one child, but everyone has a calling...to something beyond what they can do on their own. Thank you for giving us the opportunity to share our passion with you. It truly is an honor.

Matthew L. Tschirgi

Introduction
A Note from Niki

Where do I begin with this story, which was years in the making and is still being written? Probably what I should do is give you the bottom line, the broad-stroke overview that leads us to today. Adopting our six children has been the most challenging thing that we have ever done, and yet the most rewarding. Over the years, we have walked through very deep waters, and I'm not talking just about infertility. I'm talking about building a family from the pieces left shattered on the floor from numerous broken homes. It never leaves my mind that our family was built on a bonfire of grief and that for us to be a family, other families have been torn apart. The truth is, whether we had decided to build our family through adoption or not, our children's families of origin would still have been torn apart. This was not our doing; this was not our children's doing. Truly, our children are still rising from the ashes.

There have been times during our adoption journey when life has been almost unbearable—times when I have lain on the ground bawling or in the arms of a trusted friend, sobbing with a full-on ugly cry, sick with grief and fiercely hanging on to my faith in Jesus Christ as my children walked through the fire that their pasts have lit in them. I share this with you because in this book, I will not talk in detail about what I call our open-ocean times, when we tread for dear life with no shore in sight. We have had many of those times and we have always, always found land. Once washed ashore, however, one is awfully tired. My children's troubles, stories, heartaches, and failures will not be found in the pages of this book. Those are their stories, and I will protect those stories fiercely. What I do share in these pages is the building of a family through adoption, including the struggles, laughter, moments of delight, incredibly complex journey, and perseverance involved in adopting a child. You see, adoption and foster care are not for the faint of heart. I don't say this to raise myself onto a pedestal of hero worship; I merely say this because I have learned it to be true. Adoption is a hard road for everyone involved—and I do mean everyone.

There is no "I'll just adopt a baby; then there will be no problems." No, I'm sorry. That baby was in someone else's womb—most likely a traumatic womb—for nine months and quite possibly was born with drugs in its system, maybe after poor prenatal care, stress, alcohol, and more. Those things matter; those things have an effect. There will be things that you will need to work through and love your child through even if you adopt a baby. You will most likely not be able to traditionally parent the children you adopt, because your children may have post-traumatic stress disorder, sensory or attachment issues, learning disabilities, medical issues, ADHD, or any other number of challenges. I strongly suggest that anyone considering adoption or foster care read *Adopting the Hurt Child* and *Parenting the Hurt Child*, by Gregory Keck and Regina Kupecky, as well as *The Connected Child*, by Dr. Karyn Purvis. These are excellent books, and I believe they are necessary to read before bringing a child into your home.

With adoption, what becomes immediately evident is that you will always share your children. Always. They will always have birth families. Some of them may have siblings, who may live with you, with their birth family, or with another adoptive family. When you bring home your adopted child, you don't sweep the child's past under the carpet—or at least you shouldn't. Your child's past happened and is an important piece of his or her history and future. From the moment you receive your child into your home, you are building a new life and new memories, but the old life and old memories still exist. Sometimes you may even have contact with your child's birth family. In our experience, it has all been good and safe, because we make sure we do our best to keep it that way. We are the parents, but our children's biological families exist, and it would be foolish in the long run to pretend that they do not. All six of our children know that when the time comes, if they ever need us to help facilitate communication with birth family, we are here. That decision is theirs, and we always put what is in their best interest first. At times, that has meant disappointing birth family. Regardless, we honor our children and where they are on their journeys.

People may question your judgment, parenting, and sanity. That's okay. Some have questioned ours. They don't have to raise your kids; you do. Oh, and as an adoptive parent or foster parent, you have just become an educator for life. People will ask you if those are your "real kids," who your kids' "real parents" are, if your kids are "real siblings," or if you "have any of your own." I learned right from the beginning that most people aren't trying to hurt you but simply don't know, are incredibly nosy, or are perhaps a little of both. Often, I have rephrased the question into something light like "Do you mean are any of my kids biologically mine? No, they are all adopted, and I am 100 percent mom," or "Oh, do you mean who are their birth parents? Well, that's their story to tell, but what I can tell you is that children who come in to foster care have most likely experienced a combination of abuse, neglect, and trauma," or "Oh, do you mean are they birth siblings? No, but they are brothers through and through. You should see them fight over the Xbox!"

Regardless of our walks (yes, plural) through adversity, strong opinions, insensitive comments, hysterical laughter, and crying, I wouldn't change anything. I know that each child in our home is supposed to be here. I have learned and changed much from our initial placement more than fourteen years ago. I am not the same person, and for that, I am grateful. I am more compassionate, prayerful, and loving, and much wiser than I was, knowing that I have loads further to go in growth and maturity. I look at the me in the mirror today and know that I wouldn't be the woman or the mother I am currently without having gone through every scorching trial and mountaintop experience that this journey has brought us through. My heart is full. It has grown. It has enlarged. It has stretched. It has, somewhat surprisingly, stayed whole and continues to expand to this day. Why? Because I dared to open it up and let in children who have grabbed on to me, pulled me in every direction, and proven to me that I truly do have an endless capacity to love. Go ahead, kids, stretch-mark my heart.

Preface

Twinkle, Twinkle, Little Starfish

A story by Loren Eiseley is very near and dear to my heart, and I just can't seem to let go of it: "The Star Thrower" (or "Starfish Story"). The story is about an older man walking along the beach who spies in the distance a young man who appears to be dancing. As he draws closer, the older man notices that the young man isn't dancing but is rather reaching down to pick up starfish to throw back into the ocean. You see, the tide is up and the sun is out, meaning certain death for the starfish, so with great purpose, the young man keeps reaching down again and again to return the starfish to sea. The older man wonders why the young man would go to so much trouble for a few starfish when there are miles and miles of beach and too many starfish to count, and he tells the young man that he can't possibly make a difference. At that, the young man bends down, picks up a starfish, throws it into the water, then turns to the older man and says, "It made a difference for that one."

Many times on our adoption journey and even now, post-adoption, I have felt overwhelmed by the enormity of need for kids to have homes. In the state of Washington, the need is greater than the supply, and it is easy to have the perspective of the old man in "The Star Thrower." We look out over our state of Washington and see more than 10,000 children in foster care, with more than 2,100 of these children waiting for adoptive families. With so many kids waiting for adoption, we look at ourselves and wonder what kind of difference we can make. What is one more adoption when so many are in need? Does it really make a difference? And won't the tide go out again and again and again, leaving starfish stranded every day?

Perhaps you don't have the perspective of the old man but rather of the young one, reaching out and adopting. You may have adopted one, two, three, or more, and you're telling people about the need and know that each life you touch makes a difference even if you can't touch them all. Even if you can't reach them all. Even if you know that tomorrow, more children will come into foster care and more will come up for adoption, you know that you made a difference to "that one."

That is a good perspective to have, and one I advocate for sure, but there is another perspective that we need to take on: the perspective of the starfish. Instead of being the old man not understanding or the young man reaching down and picking up, maybe we should be the starfish on the shore looking up, hoping that the hand is reaching for us. When we get that perspective, that every starfish is a child and that every starfish is hoping and that every starfish we touch makes a difference, then we are driven to action.

The kids who are waiting are not a bunch of nameless and faceless children. If, like the old man, we look and see 10,000 faces all in a blur, we can walk away. But when we stop, as the young man did, and look down and see names and faces and hear hopes and dreams and get to know their stories, we can't walk away. We must stop. We must reach. Change started with one young man stopping and making a difference to one starfish...and then another and another. What if others joined the young man on the beach and reached? How many more starfish could be saved? How many more could know the difference? The starfish are waiting. They are waiting for you and for me.

1.

Infertility

S tatistics tell us that around 15 percent of couples in the United States are infertile. Male infertility plays a role in half of these couples, so I estimate that around 7 or 8 percent of the population fall into the male-infertility category. That's not a terribly large number, but it is a terribly *lonely* number. Loneliness was the number-one emotion we experienced in dealing with infertility as a couple— not anger, not grief, not hopelessness. We were surrounded by friends and acquaintances who did not know what it was like to not carry a child, nor understand the decision-making process we went through in choosing how to build our family. There were so many people, so many opinions. Most people wanted to help; I know that. People counsel you based on their own experience. I do that, too. The truth is, however, that whatever decision you make, you have to live with it—not the person with the opinion. You.

Two years into our marriage, I had finally worn my husband down to the idea of pregnancy—not that he didn't want children, but he was, and still is, a practical man. When we married, we were both working jobs that paid $5.00 an hour and neither of us had health insurance. We lived in a tiny one-bedroom apartment off the University of Idaho campus, sharing one car. I walked the two miles to work at a local coffeehouse. Every penny counted. By the time we had been married for two years, Matt had a job with benefits, so starting a family seemed more within our reach. Besides, it could take a while to get pregnant after going off birth control, so likely it would be another year or two before we had ourselves a baby.

Six months passed. Then a year. I wasn't too concerned. Perhaps it was just taking more time for us than for others. I set up a doctor's appointment and expressed my concerns to my doctor about my inability to get pregnant. He brushed them off lightly: I was a healthy young woman and everything was normal; give it another year, and if I was still not pregnant, come back.

Meanwhile, I had friends getting pregnant. One friend of mine was also struggling with conceiving, but she had a known medical condition and knew what her hurdle was. Mine, if I was even calling it a hurdle, was muddled, unclear, and, quite simply, foggy and vague. There was nothing wrong with me that I was aware of, yet something niggled my heart. If there was nothing wrong with me, then why wasn't I pregnant?

Another year went by with no baby. We had been trying to conceive for two years now. Surely, *surely,* in those twenty-four months, we should have gotten it "right." I was taking my temperature to determine ovulation. I had notes, for crying out loud! The niggling persisted. This time when I went to the doctor, I would be more assertive. Two years is a long time to wait to see what happens. The doctor finally agreed with my wondering: Based on my health history, conception shouldn't be an issue. Our first step would be a work-up for male infertility. Once that was ruled out, doctors could then start the process of evaluating me.

Leaving the doctor's office, I knew I wasn't ready for answers. After all this time and longing for a child, I wasn't ready to know if one of us was infertile.

"Alright, let's get tested," Matt said as we headed out to the car from that appointment.

"I'm not ready," I replied.

As I purposefully strode with my head pointing forward, I could feel Matt carefully glancing over at me and I knew he was putting together his response.

"Okay. We will do this together, and when you are ready, we will start with me."

As I sighed in relief, we let the day go. The ball was in my court.

Six months later, I was ready.

Cashing in on our referral to the urologist, we set up an appointment to get Matt checked out. I honestly didn't give it a second thought; this appointment was simply procedure to rule him out before we moved on to me. It was simply a stepping-stone we would have to endure to move on to the next appointment.

To say I was unprepared for the news we received that day would be an understatement. I was blindsided. Taken aback. Caught off guard. Dumbfounded. It was information that came at me so fast and with such a feeling of finality that I didn't quite know what to do with it.

We were sitting in the examination room, waiting for the doctor. After a few minutes had passed, the door opened quickly. We were grateful for the short wait time. The doctor, after quietly shutting the door, shared with us, within the space of ten seconds, devastating news that would change our lives forever: We couldn't have kids. As if at the snap of a finger, our world tilted, and I wasn't sure how it would ever be upright again. I had been expecting a long, drawn-out process of trying to figure out why we weren't getting pregnant but of eventually conceiving and having a family. I had not been expecting a quick "here's why you're not pregnant, and to top that off, you won't be pregnant—at least not on your own, and maybe not ever."

"So, there is nothing we can do? Are you telling us we can't have kids?" I blurted out.

"Not without help."

"What kind of help?"

"Not without in vitro fertilization."

Within the window of a short doctor's appointment, the trajectory of our life was knocked off course, and we stumbled to right ourselves as we sifted through the information being handed us. We had our answer for our lack of conception. There was no more searching. There was no more wondering. But now what would we do? What were our next steps?

Walking out of the hospital, I assumed that my husband was in a fragile state. What man wouldn't be? He was the reason we could not have kids. Was he wondering what this meant for our marriage? Was he worried that I would leave him? Was he questioning his manhood? I knew I needed to tread carefully on this delicate and extremely touchy topic. I loved him, and this just meant we were going to go about having a family a little differently than we had first thought. I vowed then and there not to say anything that would belittle him or threaten our union. This wasn't his fault. Although I didn't know exactly how our family would come about, I knew that somehow, someway, we would be parents.

Over the next week or two, we explored our possibilities. We quickly considered and rejected using a sperm donor. We weren't comfortable bringing in another party to create a biological child; in our hearts, we felt like it added another person to our marriage. Many people have benefited from using sperm donors and have built beautiful families. That is their journey, but this was ours, and we needed to find our own way. We began researching in vitro fertilization—specifically the cost, the process, and the odds of getting pregnant. We discussed the hard questions—which, frankly, you need to discuss: *What if we spend $18,000–$30,000 and don't get pregnant? What if, on the first round of in vitro, we have ten viable embryos and have three implanted and they all take? Then we have seven embryos remaining. Are we willing to freeze them forever or to implant them? What do we do with the lives we've* *created?* These questions mulled around in our heads, and they are good questions. They are challenging questions. They are questions only we could answer for us. We know couples who have wonderful children from in vitro fertilization, and that had been right for them. What was right for us?

Overlaying all our research was the discussion of adoption. Adoption was not a last choice or a last option for us but was woven through all our study regarding infertility. Adoption is a major theme of the Bible, intertwined throughout the book and solidly in the center of God's redemption story. We are adopted as God's children. We are commanded to care for the orphans and the widows. We are instructed to help the needy and the less fortunate. Gathering information was part of the process of coping with infertility. Through that gathering, we found peace. Peace was what led us during that time, and in the subsequent years. Deciding the course to take regarding our infertility didn't take us very long. Adoption was heavy on our hearts; we knew which way to go.

Now that we knew what route to pursue, we began to knock on doors regarding adoption. We began to gather more specific information. We knew one family in Central Washington who had adopted out of foster care, so we arranged a quick road trip to have lunch with their family and talk about the process. We learned that with foster care, there were no guarantees of adoption but fees were subsidized by the government and support was available for the kids. Plus, there were many kids who needed loving and safe homes. Next, we looked in to private adoption, but the price tag was daunting, like the price tag on in vitro fertilization was daunting. Our journey was not all about the money, but finances did play a part in our decision making, and when we were gathering information, we gathered all we could to make the best decision for us.

What you decide to do with infertility, in the end, is truly only your decision. As the sun goes down, day turns to night, and your head hits the pillow, you must be able to answer the tough questions. You must not only be able to answer them but must also be able to live with those answers. You must find your peace. We chose adoption. Others choose assisted reproduction, while some choose childlessness or simply waiting. You must choose what is right for you.

During this time, many well-meaning people offered their advice—advice we considered but felt no obligation to follow. Something had happened deep in our spirits when this curve ball had smacked us in the gut. Gone were the young adults who had been swayed by opinions and off-the-cuff advice. In their place was a hurting couple that had gotten a tangible dose of grief and of life's difficult disappointments. Whatever decision we made regarding building our family, we would have to live with. We were determined to follow our peace—and our peace, we discovered, rested solely in adoption.

Word soon spread among our friends that we were pursuing adoption, and before the week was over, someone pulled me aside with their passionate point of view. "I know you are considering adoption, but do you know you can have your own kid?"

On and on they went about having our own kid while I sat there staring at them, thinking, *Why the heck does your idea about how our family should happen mean so much to you? Do you have to pay for in vitro fertilization? No. Do you have to go through hormone treatment? No. Do you have to live with our decision? No.* It was jarring to me, how passionate they were about my life, and why it mattered so much to them that we were choosing adoption, like it wasn't the best decision or wasn't good enough. *Good thing God doesn't think like that about adopting His children into the Kingdom.* I probably should have said that out loud. I politely excused myself and found that the conversation had solidified our decision in my mind: Adoption wasn't second best. For them, maybe; for us, no. Adoption was our *first choice.*

Not really knowing what we were doing, we contacted the State of Washington to find out what we needed to do to become foster parents. Pursuing adoption through the Department of Social and Health Services (DSHS) was where we started, based on the experience of our friends who had adopted through them. After only one phone call, we found out when the foster-parenting classes would be offered, and we signed up. After connecting with another couple in our church who were struggling with infertility, we carpooled to another town for forty hours of training over the summer. Though we were overwhelmed with paperwork, home studies, interviews, CPR classes, HIV/AIDS training, background checks, fingerprinting, etc., we did what we had to do. That's what you do when you want something. When you want your dream. When you want something to come to pass. You work for it.

That fall, we were licensed in the State of Washington as foster parents. After all that work, we finally understood what foster care was all about. It was about reunifying families and, if that wasn't possible, pursuing adoption, first with relatives and then, if that wasn't possible, with non-relatives. During one of the classes, our trainer passed around a picture of two older boys who were coming up for adoption. When that picture landed in our friend's hand, she stared at it, a peculiar light coming into her eyes. I knew she knew. She knew, right then and there, that those boys were her boys. And she was right. They adopted those boys—and, later, their little brother—and then went on to miraculously have two biological children. With adoption, sometimes you know right away.

We, on the other hand, were confused. Why had we gotten licensed as foster parents when our goals at the time were so different? Our goal was to adopt a baby and build our family. The goal of foster care was to reunify kids with their birth families.

What do you do with two different goals? You regroup. You find another goal that matches yours. Putting foster care on hold, much to the chagrin of DSHS, who needed us as foster parents immediately, we found an open-adoption agency in Spokane that worked only with infertile couples and had no recurring fees—meaning if an adoption fell through, the fees would apply to the next adoption, until you had a child permanently placed with you. That seemed fair and right. Kids need homes, and this couple needed a kid. We weren't sure where the money was going to come from (at the time, the cost was around $18,000), but we trusted our peace and chose to move forward.

Starting over, we began the process of another home study. We had just gotten licensed with the State of Washington, and now we were getting licensed with a private agency. We were gluttons for paperwork punishment. This time around, we had to create an adoption portfolio, which is a book you make about yourself with pictures and information so the birth mom can get to know you, to see if you would be a good fit for her child.

I felt like we were interviewing for a job. In some ways, we were. The job of being parents.

Meanwhile, as we plowed through more paperwork, we communicated our openness to taking in foster kids for short-term care, just no permanent placements. There was another foster family in our church, and we did respite care (temporary care for children in foster care) for their two boys when they needed help. This allowed us to get our feet wet at this parenting thing and also help our community. We were praying for a child by Christmas, and we were trying to find contentment in waiting—because that's what you do most of the time with adoption. You wait.

Finished with our second home study, we became licensed with our private agency. We were now licensed in two places, and more than ready to be parents. We had all the paperwork and training to prove it.

November passed into December, with no word from either agency. I wasn't surprised about not being contacted by Foster-to-Adopt through DSHS, which places a child in your home when the child is close to having parental rights relinquished or terminated, or has had them relinquished or terminated and is up for adoption.

After all, we were in a very small town, with a very small pool of kids available to adopt. We also knew our private agency in Spokane was dependent on birth moms coming to them, and then birth moms choosing us. It could be days, or it could be a year. Again, the waiting.

Part way through December, my phone rang, and on the other end of the line was a social worker from DSHS. "Niki, you aren't going to believe this. I have the perfect adoption case for you. Just perfect. All your dreams are coming true."

Excitedly, my mind went into overdrive. By some miracle, did DSHS have a baby for us? Or twins? I had heard of babies being brought to hospitals or fire stations. Maybe that's what had happened. They knew we were not doing long term-foster care yet because we wanted a baby and were waiting on a call from our agency in Spokane.

"Okay, what do you have for us?" I asked.

"Well, I have two boys for you. They are ages seven and nine. In fact, you have done respite for them! They are going to be coming up for adoption and need a home."

My heart sank. Why had she told me all my dreams were coming true? My dream was to have a baby, but here she was, offering me two older boys coming up for adoption. They weren't even up for adoption yet.

"Umm, I need to talk to Matt," I said.

She agreed and wanted to hear back from me as soon as we had made our decision.

I called Matt, who felt the same hesitancy I did. We weren't opposed to older-child adoption, but we were becoming first-time parents and were pretty set on a baby. Dang it, I couldn't have a baby. The only way I was getting a baby was through adoption, so I held out in my heart, but felt unsure of what to do. I felt bad that we weren't jumping all over taking these kids who needed a home, but we were so uncertain. Was this how we would always feel when we got a call with such a monumental decision attached?

When I shared my concerns with some coworkers, the opinions flowed again. "But you've been praying to have kids by Christmas! Look! Kids! Before Christmas!"

That was true, but there was also the matter of praying God's will. Was it God's will that we have kids before Christmas, or simply our desire? I fully confess that I have prayed for things I wanted while not necessarily being sure they were in God's will. At the end of the day, my prayer needed to be "Thy will be done."

Not knowing what else to do, I called Matt again and asked him to take a prayer walk at lunch to seek God for an answer to what we should do about these two boys. I was confused, and somebody needed to hear from God—and it wasn't going to be me, apparently. I was completely immobilized by the request. He agreed to take the prayer walk.

Later that afternoon, Matt called me with his answer. "Niki, I took that prayer walk you asked me to take, and while I was praying, God spoke to my heart. I heard, 'If you take these kids, you will miss the baby I have for you.'"

Mulling over his deep soul impression, I said, "Then it is pretty clear that we need to say no to these boys."

Immediately, I made the unpopular call to the social worker to say that no, we would not be taking the boys. I could tell she wasn't happy with me, but I was at peace with our decision. I also remembered that we were the ones who had to live with our decision, not her, and I could live with this one. God had spoken clearly to my husband. We would be doing a disservice to the kids if we said yes. They were not meant for us. I no longer felt uncertain. I felt sure.

A few months later, we found out that the "perfect" adoption case never became an adoption; the boys had gone home to their biological family. Because of the time frame, if we would have taken the two boys, we would not have gotten the later call for our son, because our licensed home would have been full with the two boys. We would have missed the baby God had for us, just like He had said we would. We also wouldn't have adopted the boys, because they went back to their biological family. We would have missed *everything*. The disappointment of our social worker and of those who had thought we should take the kids was nothing compared to the disappointment we would have felt at never having our baby.

2.

Alex

Tapping my fingers at my desk, I was *beyond* distracted. Waiting for "the call" from our adoption agency had me on the edge of my seat. We had done everything possible up to this point. There was nothing else to do. All our paperwork, payments, and photographs were on file. The only thing left to do was wait. Would it be hours? Days? Months? Years?

"Unacceptable," I whispered under my breath. We had been through so much already. We had put numerous hours of training, plus blood, sweat, and tears, into the process of becoming parents. In my frantic opinion, we couldn't wait years. Waiting months was killing me, but I really didn't have a choice. Deep down, I wanted what was best. I wanted the right child to be in our home, for our sakes and theirs. But that didn't mean waiting was easy.

Tapping my fingers some more, I stared at the pile of papers I had to file. After straightening them into a neat little heap, I moved on to organizing my pens and pencils. One minute passed, but it felt more like ten. Time dragged on. Wiping down the counters, sweeping the floors, and cleaning the glass in the office of our church, where I was a receptionist, brought the slow turn of the clock. At least with a pregnancy, you have a clear window of delivery. With adoption, it is anyone's guess.

Plopping back down on my seat, I inhaled a few deep breaths. Then, closing my eyes, I exhaled a whispered prayer. "Lord, let the next phone call be the call telling me I have a baby."

Opening my eyes, I stared at the telephone and felt a strange awareness in my body. The best I can describe the feeling is as a deep knowing. I felt a greater amount of faith than I could have imagined. I hadn't put it there; I felt a faith and a knowing that could only come from above.

Did I dare to believe the knowing? I surrendered tentatively to the knowing, but I was done waiting. I was ready. I believed in the power of the prayer I had prayed.

Ring, ring.

I stared at the phone.

Ring, ring.

I stared some more.

Ring, ring.

Trembling, I reached out and picked up the receiver. "Good morning, this is Niki. How may I help you?" I said as normally as possible.

"Niki?"

"Yes, this is she."

There was a pause, then a chuckle. "How would you like to have a baby?"

Silence. I sat in complete silence for two heartbeats.

"Yes," I whispered.

Incredulous. That was what I was. I had just prayed that the next phone call would be "the call."

Finding my voice, I said with more conviction, "Yes. Why yes, I would like to have a baby. When?"

I asked when because usually, a birth mother picked the family who would be adopting her child sometime around the sixth or seventh month of her pregnancy, and the adoptive family would meet the birth mom and often be there for the delivery.

I heard laughter on the other end of the phone again. "What I meant was, would you like to have a baby now. Like, right now."

"What do you mean, right now?"

"I mean that we have a four-week-old baby here right now, and the birth mother wants you and Matt to be his parents. So I mean right now."

"Tell me more! Yes, I want him!"

Joyful laughing tinkled over the phone. "Well, his name is Alex, and he is a beautiful baby boy. His birth mom knows that she cannot keep him. He is currently in foster care here in the Spokane area, which works out perfectly for you because you are not only licensed with us but also with the State of Washington as a foster parent, so they can transfer his case to you."

Ahhhh...so that's why we got licensed as foster parents first!

"What do you need us to do?" I asked.

"You and Matt need to come up to the agency and meet the birth family, and then from there we will work on transferring Alex's case to you and, probably within a month or so, placing him for adoption through our agency."

"Thank you. Yes, I'll call Matt and tell him. You tell us when to be there, and we will be there."

"Okay, I'll get back to you. Congratulations, Niki. Now get on the phone and call Matt!"

"I will! Good-bye!"

Slouching in my chair, totally relaxed, with my head thrown back, legs sprawled forward, and a huge grin on my face, I just sat for a moment. My mind was a jumble of excitement, awe, and intense emotions. We had a baby. We finally had a baby. I was going to be a mom.

Shooting up in my chair to sit ramrod straight, I glanced once again at the phone that had just delivered the news I had been waiting for. Deliberately closing my eyes, I whispered the most heartfelt and simplest prayer I had every prayed.

"Thank you."

3.

Open Adoption

Our agency was set up in an old renovated home north of historic downtown Spokane, welcoming and homey to all who entered. Standing in the doorway of the agency, Matt and I felt the current of electricity pass between us. This was it. Today, we would get to see pictures of our baby, Alex, and meet his birth family.

Our adoption counselor ushered us in with her broad smile and encouraged us to hang up our coats. "The family is already here, upstairs, waiting for you. There is no rush. They were early, and eager to meet you."

We had very little information about Alex's birth family, yet they had a whole book on us. We knew that Alex's birth mom was young and the situation heartbreaking; based on her home life and other circumstances, there was nobody capable of raising Alex. Because Alex's birth grandmother knew her rights and the rights of her daughter, she knew that even though Alex was currently in foster care, they had the right to place him for adoption with a family of their choosing through a private agency, with hope for contact as he grew up.

On a side note, originally, we had picked out baby names because we had been told that we would meet the birth mother beforehand and most likely could name our baby, but with Alex already born and named, we hesitated about changing his given name, for his sake and his birth mom's sake. Naming is a powerful thing.

He was born Alex Paul, so we decided to alter it slightly, to Alexander Steven Walter (his middle names are after my late father), and still call him Alex. More than a decade later, we see the strength in naming, as our fourteen-year-old son insists on being called Alex, not Alexander. His name, he tells us, is Alex, and he gets miffed sometimes when we call him Alexander. Never underestimate the influence of your child's development in the womb, or of that which has been spoken over them. I knew of one adoptive mom who changed her daughter's name at birth and later watched as her daughter named her dolls the name she had been given at birth, without ever knowing that her name had been changed. I'm not telling anyone that they should (or shouldn't) change their adoptive child's name. Just food for thought. Every child is different. Every situation is different.

Back at the agency, glancing up the stairs to where our future lay, we hesitated only a moment before ascending into the unknown and the realization of parenthood. Our counselor opened the door, and as we entered the waiting room, birth grandma, birth mom, and two birth aunts nervously stood up and cautiously moved toward us. Grandma shook our hands first. Looking deeply into her clear caramel eyes, I recognized a profound and brewing grief that belied the gentle smile on her face. Resignation to the circumstance had brought them here.

Warmly, she held on to my hand and immediately began to speak to us about, astonishingly, us. "We picked you because of the picture on the front page of your adoption book."

Raising my eyebrows and smiling even more broadly at her as she released my hand, I felt my nerves melt away and any awkwardness subside. "Really? We had been ice-skating that day, and a friend had captured us leaning in to each other and laughing on the rink as we tried to stay upright."

"Yes. It was your smile, Niki. You reminded me of my daughter. I caught a glimpse of her in you, and we knew that you two were supposed to be Alex's parents."

Humbled by the process of selection, I hugged her. What else do you say or do for someone giving you their grandson?

Quietly, Alex's birth mom waited to meet us, and ever so shyly, with her head ducked, she peeked up at us from under her curly hair. This young girl had recently been through a traumatic birth, delivering Alex by emergency C-section, and then had him whisked off to a foster home. I could perceive the uncertainty in her gaze. Her mother had spearheaded the movement toward open adoption, doing everything in her limited power to give her daughter a choice in where her son went.

"We have pictures to show you," piped up a young voice in the room.

Turning to Alex's birth mom's twin sister, I smiled and introduced myself to her, shaking her hand sincerely. "We would love to see pictures!"

Gingerly, we all sat down in our group of six, and pictures were produced and explained. The third sister, who now felt more comfortable, pointed out details and described what was happening in some of the pictures.

As I laid eyes on Alex for the first time, my heart leapt and water sprang from my eyes. He was exactly what my heart desired. I had not been brave enough to pray for specifics for my baby, because I had felt it would be selfish to ask. Wasn't it enough that I would at some point be getting a baby? But there, before me, on the crinkled photograph, was the secret vision of my heart that had not passed my lips. Apparently, it hadn't had to, for God truly did know the desires of my heart.

Gazing back at me from the photograph with wide brown eyes and a wild shock of brown hair was Alex. That hair. I had secretly longed for a baby with wild and unruly hair, and there he was.

"He's perfect," I said.

Smiling, Alex's birth family showed us other pictures of him in the hospital and with his birth mom—all pieces to our son's life, which we had yet to experience. Pieces of his life that I would tuck away for him. His history.

"These are for you," they told me, handing over the original Polaroid pictures for me to keep. I could see that although it was hard for them, they were happy to meet us and happy that they had the power to choose where Alex would go. It made them sad that we could not have babies, and happy to know that they could be the ones to give us a family. Through our shared grief, maybe we could help each other heal.

Realization came over me at that moment. This was open adoption.

At first, I had been terrified and a little displeased by the thought of open adoption. What did that mean? Would I still be mom? Would my child be confused? I hadn't wanted to share what we had so longed for. It wasn't fair! Other moms and dads just took their babies home from the hospital, but I would have to share my baby for the rest of his life? I had originally bristled inwardly at the thought.

Eventually, I bent outwardly as I began to understand what open adoption was truly about. Surprisingly, what I learned was that open adoption was shared *relationship*, not shared *roles*. I was Mom; Matt was Dad; these women who would continue to be in Alex's life were, simply put, more people to love him. My fear that had been fueled by the unknown morphed into understanding. We would be a part of the healing that would need to come in the next weeks, months, and years for these women, just as they would be a part of ours.

All my lingering fears about open adoption evaporated after our meeting with Alex's birth family. They weren't trying to intrude or to take something from us. They simply wanted to be a respectful part of Alex's life, and it was very plain to see they were taking nothing but giving everything.

Two hours later, we were exiting the agency, knowing that our meeting had gone well and had confirmed to the family that yes, we were the ones. My heart expanded a bit more to make room for these new people in our lives. One never knows what will happen when opening oneself to new and different things. I'd like to think that the simple act of saying yes and walking through the door to our agency that day, not knowing what to expect, allowed for the enlargement to take place. I know I didn't will the change; maybe the change happened because I offered it. Maybe the change willed me.

Overflowing with excitement about setting a date to pick up Alex, we headed home to wait for a few more days. We would be picking him up from the DSHS office on May 1. Our baby was almost home. My heart had been full of the idea of him, and now it was full of a vision of him. My heart was full of unruly, wild hair and four heartbroken yet hopeful women.

4.

Little Brown Eyes

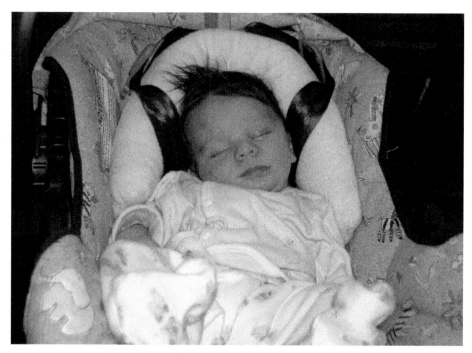

Alex (4 weeks old) on his first day with us, May 1, 2003.

Peering into the room that would soon be our son's, I was glad I had gotten the nursery completed. Some friends had cautioned me about decorating a nursery, that it might cause me pain, but I'd had to do something during my aching time of waiting. When you are pregnant, you have a due date; when you are adopting, you have a due sometime. I had known I would get a baby; I just hadn't known when. I had been okay with my nursery sitting empty, knowing that it would not be empty forever. The little gestures from my family had helped me stay afloat as we had waited for our call for a baby. My mom mailed me Martha Stewart burp cloths, and my auntie and cousin in Wisconsin sewed me an adorable red-and-blue ducky blanket. I remember rubbing its softness against my cheek and imagining the blanket covering my baby. These gifts that had come without warning in the mail were more than just baby items; they had been hope. I was done protecting my heart from hurt. You must risk moving forward, and so I had.

This would be the last time I would open my nursery door to emptiness. Lying before me were now Alex's lovely yellow walls bordered with happy sailboats. It was no longer just "the future baby's" room. It was Alex's room. My best friend had dutifully come over and helped me paint the walls and hang my border and curtains, patiently and prayerfully waiting alongside me for our coveted phone call. Adoption tends to do that, pull people into your story and keep them there—quite a beautiful thing, really.

A white crib was set up in the corner, with gingham yellow-and-white-checked sheets and, of course, the ducky fleece blanket from my auntie and cousin draped over the railing. My mother-in-law had sewn sailboat curtains and a matching child-size blanket to adorn the room. Looped around the crib railing was a charming bendy giraffe waiting to delight the crib's occupant. Over in the other corner was a white changing table and mattress with yellow pad. We even had stocked some diapers and wet wipes. We were ready, right?

Closing the door to the room, I guessed that I was as ready as I was going to be. Ready or not, we were picking up our baby that day. We were picking up Alex.

Driving up to Spokane felt different this time around. There was an air of expectancy, anticipation, and an aura of surreality. Glancing back over my left shoulder, I looked at the empty car seat buckled in to the back of our Subaru Outback. In just a few hours, we would be meeting Alex and securing him in there, right there in that car seat. This was truly and really happening!

After we arrived at the DSHS building off Atlantic Avenue, Matt removed the car seat from the bucket base and grabbed my hand. We would go in as two, and we would come out as three. We would go in as a couple, and we would come out as a family.

Entering the office, we were met by an upset but gracious woman. She introduced herself as Alex's foster mom and, fighting back tears, she handed me a present, a Mother's Day card, and a bouquet of flowers. "I've brought all of Alex's things for you. They are right here in these boxes. I just had to come in here and meet you. I had to know where he was going. I am so glad to know he is going to a family who cannot have children, and to a family who loves the Lord."

Overwhelmed, I looked at her. I had heard that the foster mom was upset that she wasn't going to be able to keep Alex. She had been told by her social worker that because of the nature of the case, Alex would be a "slam dunk" adoption, that she would be able to adopt Alex. Sadly, for her, it turned out not to be the case. I felt badly for her, but as a fellow foster mom, I knew that there were no guarantees in adoption and that until paperwork is signed on the dotted line, nothing is for sure.

We had heard that Alex's foster mom may or may not show up but that we should expect her not to. But there she was, bravely—if not without agitation—handing over Alex to the social worker and showering me with gifts in the process. The kindness she shared through her own pain was a touching, but slightly unnerving, tribute to our day. Matt and I knew Alex was meant for us, and we knew she had other children. We knew that in time, it would be okay; however, we also knew it was hard, and we respected the moment.

The social worker ushered us back into a small room, and we sat down with her and got our first tangible look at Alex. As he snuffled contentedly in a car seat on the floor, his wild hair sticking straight up, I drank him in—and boy, was I thirsty. Gingerly, I bent down, placed my hands carefully under his armpits and lifted his little face up to mine. He was dressed in white and yellow pajamas, and as I breathed him in, he kicked his little feet and snuffled some more. He was perfect.

Lightly, I cradled my son against my shoulder. My son. I had a son. Reality had not set in. But it had to be reality, because the social worker was carrying on like business as usual while she finalized paperwork and asked for signatures.

Reluctantly, I handed Alex over to Matt, who eagerly took his new son in his hands. Dad. Matt was a dad. Was this what it felt like in the hospital after one gave birth? Probably not exactly. I didn't know, and it didn't matter. We had just become parents in a most unorthodox way.

Signing my name on the paperwork, I handed the pen back over to Matt and readily took my son back into my arms. That was it. Alex's case in the foster care system, as of May 1, 2003, was officially transferred to us. After one month, his case would be transferred to our adoption agency, and then we would begin the process of finalizing his adoption.

Saying our good-byes to the social worker, we headed back out to the car. How dreamlike it was to unlock our car and buckle Alex into his car seat! Driving across the city to Matt's mom's house, Matt played chauffer as I sat in the back with our son. I kept sending sidelong looks over at Alex, who sat sweetly with his little brown eyes watching the world go by. This was crazy! Our life had just altered forever. Looking ahead at Matt peacefully driving, I relished the truth of our new roles. Mom. Dad. Son. On the first of May, our hearts almost bursting, we officially became a family. We had been delivered a son. The gaping hole in my heart had been filled. Healing had begun.

5.

Big Brown Eyes

Carlosse (age 2) and I meeting for the first time, December 24, 2003.

After the finalization of Alex's adoption (he was seven months old to the day), we decided to get the ball rolling to adopt again. This time around, we decided to pursue foster-to-adopt. It had taken about a year from our very first appointment with our adoption agency to Alex being officially ours. We knew it could take months, maybe even years, to get a call for a legally free child under the age of three from DSHS. (A legally free child in the foster care system is a child who has had parental rights relinquished or terminated and is ready to be adopted.) By the time they become legally free, a lot of kids are already in homes that have been fostering them, or they are with relatives who end up adopting. We knew our odds of getting a call right away were slim at best, especially in our small town of Pullman, Washington, so we expanded our request to the larger city of Spokane. Because we were focused on building our family, not on being foster parents, we were very specific about the age we wanted our second child to be. We didn't want a large age gap between our children.

Mailing in our form to Spokane, we began the wait while continuing to enjoy our baby. Knowing how the system worked (meaning paperwork sometimes gets lost, delayed, or ... lost), I made a follow-up call two weeks later to check on the progress of our paperwork. "Hello, this is Niki Tschirgi. I'm just following up on our paperwork for adoption in Spokane."

I was put on hold as they searched for us in their system. "I'm sorry, we don't have your paperwork," they announced.

"All right. Should I send in another form?"

"Yes, please do that."

Sending in our form a second time with a small sigh, we began the wait again. A couple of weeks passed, and we were getting ready to head up to Spokane for an adoption conference, so I called again to check on the progress of our paperwork. "Hello, this is Niki Tschirgi. I'm following up on our paperwork for adoption in Spokane. We sent in a second form because somehow, the first form didn't make it there."

"Hold on, let me check for you."

I waited as they searched for us in their system. Again.

"I'm sorry, we don't have your paperwork."

"Really?"

By this time, I was laughing. I wouldn't call it incredulous laughter—more like knowing laughter. I suppose I could have gotten really bent out of shape that our paperwork got lost not once but twice—but I knew that, regardless of what happened with DSHS, God was bigger than a paper trail, bigger than the courts, and bigger than the government. God was just plain bigger. These questions rolled around in my mind: Would we trust? Would we trust that, no matter what happened, God was in control of our destiny and we were doing what we were supposed to be doing?

Trust was the foremost thing that Matt and I learned through each adoption we pursued or that pursued us. No matter how badly we wanted a child who was already in our home, ultimately, we wanted the child who was *supposed* to be in our home more. This sometimes included saying no to a child or children when the world looked on and told us to say yes. We know that it is important to listen to your heart and be in unity with your partner. (If you don't have a partner, just listen to your heart.) If you do those two things, you will be okay...mostly.

My knowing laugh was also birthed out of something else I knew very well. I knew that foster care was, and still is, the devil's playground. The neediest, most broken, and vulnerable humans in our nation are our children in foster care. Doesn't a wolf prey on the weakest of the herd? Doesn't the lion pick off the young, wounded, and sick in the group? Of course that is where the devil will have his heyday! We never lost sight of the fact that we were in a spiritual battle every single time we accepted a foster child into our home or planned for a permanent placement through adoption.

"So, would you like me to send in my paperwork a third time?" I almost can't believe that I managed to say it without sarcasm, but I suppose my mind was on spiritual things that day.

"Yes, please."

"All right, well, we'll get it in the mail as soon as we can."

Hanging up the phone, I took a moment to get centered and possibly gain some perspective. When there are obstacles in the way, there must be something important up ahead. There are not roadblocks for nothing. Remember how I told you the foster care system is the devil's playground? The devil doesn't like any kids to leave the system and to find hope and healing. We were making movement to completely rock a child's world in a good way, and the devil wasn't going to make it easy. But he wasn't going to win, either. He might be the bully on the playground, but we were about to put him in his place.

Years later as I look back, I know this to be true: The roadblocks, dead-ends, heartbreak, and loss were the bumpy road that led to our six children. The very things that the enemy tried to use to prevent us from getting *our* children were the very things that ultimately brought us straight to them.

After work that day, as we drove up to Spokane for our adoption conference, I felt more certain than ever that we were on the right path for our next adoption. We knew we were hitting obstacles, but we also knew we had to press on and press through. The destination doesn't change just because detours send us in a different direction. Of course, we *could* turn around and go back, or give up, but we chose not to. We would never adopt another child if we stopped.

As we wandered around the booths set up at the adoption conference the next morning, I spied a Washington DSHS booth. Making a beeline for the social workers manning the booth, I stopped and told them our story about the lost paperwork. "So now I'm sending it in for a third time," I explained matter-of-factly.

"Wait just a minute," one of the women said excitedly. "I happen to have the form right here. You fill it out for me right now and hand it to me personally, and I will get it processed Monday morning."

Smiling, I gladly took her outstretched pen. Within minutes, I had filled out the familiar paperwork for the fourth time (the third copy was at home, waiting to be mailed). Finally, our paperwork had been properly received to get us in the system. Now, we simply had to do what we were good at: wait.

Gathering Alex into my arms later that week after we were back in Pullman, I stared into his deep brown eyes, nuzzled his mop of wild baby hair, and wondered who would be the next to grace our home. I really wanted a girl this time around. Would she be younger than Alex? Older? Who would she be? Would the child even be a girl?

Matt and I chose to treat every adoption like a pregnancy, not putting a gender preference on the paperwork. We did not want to limit ourselves to who might need us and whom we might need. We certainly did not want to limit God. We often mused that these were our paperwork pregnancies, or that we were going through a paper pregnancy, because seriously, when you adopt or foster, it is like nine months of paperwork. Women often teased me and said I was lucky to not have stretch marks. I usually looked unwaveringly in their eyes and said, "Maybe not on my stomach, but most certainly on my heart."

Nine days after filling out the paperwork at the adoption conference, we got the call. Not nine months...nine days.

"Niki, we have a child for you."

"What?"

"This is going to be a very unusual request. We never do this, but we are asking you to say yes or no over the phone without meeting this child."

"Oh. Um, okay. I wasn't expecting a call this soon. Can you tell me a little bit more about this child and their case?"

"Well, he's a darling little boy who is two years old, going on three in a couple of months. He has been living with a relative this whole time, and because of certain circumstances, a home study could not be completed. He is now up for adoption. He has been legally free for over a year now; he is completely ready to be placed for adoption. His name is Carlosse."

I was still stuck back on the fact that they had called me for a three-year-old. Three? I didn't know anything about raising a three-year-old! I know we had put in our paperwork a request for three years or younger, but an older child? Was this really happening? Were we ready to adopt some older child nine days after we had re-resubmitted our paperwork, and with a nine-month-old at home?

"So, what do you say? Yes? No?"

Oh, that was so like DSHS. I knew they had deadlines and needs and needed to place this child. *Can you give a girl a second? You just asked me to take a child, sight unseen, with about one minute worth of background information.* And my husband was sitting innocently at work, oblivious to what was happening and the request that had just been made of us.

Trying to wrap my head around the unexpected phone call and the terms of place-ment, I stammered out my surprised response. "Can I at least call my husband and talk it over with him?"

"Oh yes, yes. Go ahead and talk to Matt. But let us know as soon as possible!"

"Of course. We will get back to you with our answer as soon as we can."

I hung up the phone.

Was this why our paperwork was delayed? For Carlosse? I considered that thought for a moment.

Because it was so close to Christmas and a lot of children come into foster care dur-ing the holidays, there were no temporary foster homes for Carlosse to go to, so he had been placed in Sally's House up in Spokane, just waiting to be adopted, appar-ently waiting for us. (Sally's House is a lockdown facility that provides a safe place for children to live for up to ninety days after they have been removed from their homes. It is the only emergency foster care group home of its kind in Washington.)

Quickly, I called Matt at work and told him the situation we had been presented. I shared my fears that I wouldn't know how to parent an older child, about not being ready. He paused in his patient and thoughtful way and said, "This feels right. I know we have never met him, and I know that this is sudden, but this is exactly what we asked for. He needs a home, and we can give him one. Yes. Let's say yes."

As I sat quietly, attempting to absorb the information and Matt's sure answer, a scripture verse quickened in my heart: "Let the little children come to me" (Matthew 19:14).

Like a sweet and aching recollection, this verse passed through my mind and flowed over me, covering me with warmth and comfort. This was how Jesus had responded to His disciples regarding children approaching Him. Children were running up to Jesus, wanting to be with Him, but the disciples saw them as a distraction and attempted to turn them away. Jesus wasn't having it. He wanted to draw the children close to Him. That's what we were to do: let this little child come to us.

Peace settled in my heart once again. This was right. I was familiar with this peace. I hadn't felt a strong yes or a fervent no at first, just an I-don't-know and a little bit of panic, but my husband was certain, and from the verse that had just hastened to me, I was sure God was certain. Well, two out of three would have to do. We were all in this together. The decision was made. Now I, soon-to-be mom of an older child, was as certain as I was going to be in the time limit set upon us.

Enough pondering, I silently chided myself. Swiftly, I called back the social worker to let her know our decision, that yes, we wanted Carlosse, and that in two days' time, on Christmas Day, we were flying to Wisconsin for the holiday. Should we come pick him up and take him with us, or what were we to do?

"I'll tell you what. Why don't you come over to Sally's House on Christmas Eve and meet Carlosse? That way, you can at least have had a visit with him. I think it would be too much for Carlosse to be removed from his home and leave with complete strangers on a plane and then to be with more strangers for two weeks. Go on your vacation, come home for a day or two, get his room all set up, and then come up and get him. He's yours."

After packing the three of us for our trip out of state, we made our way up to Spokane, where we were spending the night with Matt's mom for Christmas Eve. After dropping Alex off with her, we drove over to Sally's House. Not knowing what to expect, we were met at the door by security and escorted through another set of intimidating lockdown doors. Staying close on the heels of the guard, we zigzagged through halls, passing an indoor swimming pool along the way, until we were finally ushered in to a small waiting room with a couch, a few chairs, and some books and toys scattered on the ground. Silently, we sat waiting to meet our new son. We had not even seen a picture of him.

Softly, the door opened, and a social worker led in a little boy with sandy-blonde hair and big brown eyes. Clutched to his chest against his canary-yellow shirt was a Spider-Man action figure. He gingerly came forward, not looking at us, clutching his toy even more tightly to his chest.

Trying to put myself in his little shoes, I imagined what this child had been through the past several days. He had been removed from the only home he knew by people he didn't know, and placed in a building he didn't know, sleeping in a bed he didn't know, and now he was meeting more people he didn't know, who were going to be his new parents. And it was Christmas Eve.

I couldn't imagine. I just couldn't. Already, this child, just shy of three, had been through more in his life than most people in our social circle.

Reaching out to him, I began to inquire about Spider-Man. His big brown eyes dared to peek up at me as his clasp on the toy became less pronounced. I had seen those eyes before, the deep, dark sadness in them. The haunting. The loss. The eyes of a child in foster care. The eyes of a child who had seen too much. Carlosse's eyes were coffee brown, and they spoke volumes to me of the hurt and the pain he had gone through. Maybe he couldn't verbalize it, but I could see it, just the same.

As I coaxed him out of his shell, he agreed to sit on my lap and then began to chatter about Spider-Man. I pulled him close to my heart, leaned my cheek on his head, and breathed deeply of his scent as I listened to his small, sweet voice. I could love this child. How was I going to leave for Wisconsin for two weeks and leave him here? But I had to. That was just the way it was. Another bump in the road of the foster care system. Another hard situation made harder.

My husband pulled out our camera to take a picture to show our family, and Carlosse turned shy again, ducking his head at the appearance of the small silver digital box.

Getting down on his knees, Matt asked Carlosse if he could take a picture of Spider-Man first.

Nodding his head bashfully, Carlosse held Spider-Man out for a picture.

After taking a picture of the toy, Matt turned the camera to Carlosse to let him inspect the photographic work. A gentle smile was coaxed from his lips, obvious pleasure at the sight of his Spider-Man captured on the screen. Perfect little teeth flashed us, and dimples appeared in his cheeks.

"Would it be okay if I took a picture of you and Spider-Man together?" Matt asked.

Nodding his head, Carlosse pulled Spider-Man close to his chest as Matt snapped another picture.

"Here. See? It's you and Spider-Man!"

This time, a big smile blossomed on Carlosse's face as he peered intently at the back of the camera where he and Spider-Man were proudly displayed. With that, he gently reclined back again on my lap with his Spider-Man close to his heart and him close to mine. Matt took a third and final picture, capturing a moment in time only the three of us experienced: our first moments with our new son.

Saying good-bye, I steeled my heart and didn't think about the fact that we were walking away from our two-year-old son. Instead, I told myself it was for a short time, he was in a safe place, and the social worker had said he was ours. My heart ached, but not with sorrow. My heart ached because it had just stretched. It had stretched again to make room for this child. It was an ache I was becoming famil-iar with. It was an ache that I loved. It was an ache I would feel time and time again—the ache of stretch marks on my heart.

6.

Carlosse

Picking up Carlosse at the DSHS office on January 9, 2004.

C hristmas in Wisconsin was wonderful and painful at the same time. We were excited to be there to see family. Showing off Alex to the great-grandparents and all the aunties, uncles, and cousins was wonderful. This was their first time seeing Alex in the flesh, and he was well loved, cuddled, smothered, and adored. Because my family was so far away, making it difficult to get together often, I reveled in the love and attention.

We passed around the picture of Carlosse and me to everyone and celebrated, but every day, I thought of my little boy waiting for us at Sally's House in Spokane. Our vacation couldn't get over soon enough.

After flying back to Spokane on January 6, 2004, we began making our way back to Pullman, knowing Carlosse was tucked away at Sally's House. Matt and I needed to unpack from our trip, get our house ready for an almost-three-year-old, go back to work for a day or two, and then head back up to Spokane to pick up Carlosse. Driving away from the city that night, I was acutely aware that I was so close, yet so far away from our son. Soon he would be home, but not soon enough.

We set up a meeting with our social worker for a few days later and then once again made our way to Spokane. This time we arrived at our social worker's office to pick up Carlosse. Our worker happily and hurriedly greeted us as we walked through the doors of the building. She was gathering up the last bit of paperwork for Carlosse.

At first, I noticed all of Carlosse's stuff, in two garbage bags, ready to take home. And then there he was, our son, sitting on the floor, looking at books. He had on too-big jeans rolled up, and a chunky striped sweater. He was clean, but I noticed he had shaggy hair and the remnants of a rattail growing out at the base of his neck. Crouching down to his level, I greeted him and watched as he quietly flipped through the pages of his book. I gently guided him up onto his feet, and then we walked over to a chair, where I pulled him onto my lap and opened his book for him to continue looking through. Finally, we were together again.

"I just need you to sign some paperwork, and then you can be off. I told Carlosse he was going on a trip with you."

Matt and I looked at each other, and I could tell exactly what he was thinking: *A trip? That poor kid. Every time we tell him he's going to go on a trip, will he think he is moving to a new family?* We silently communicated that we would expound on that little statement after Carlosse got in the car.

With everything in order, Matt gathered up Carlosse's belongings, and with Alex tucked on one of my hips and Carlosse's hand firmly in mine, we left the social worker's office and made our way to the car. Strapping Alex into his car seat and then buckling Carlosse into his, I marveled once again at my family. I had two sons in the back seat of my car. Just like that.

"Now, Carlosse, I know the social worker told you that you were going to go on a trip with us, but it's more than just a trip. You are going to come live with us forever. We are going to be your new family," Matt explained.

Glancing back at Carlosse sitting in the back seat, I watched as he absorbed this new information about being a part of our family. His countenance was serene, not resigned—like it wasn't news but was right for him to be our son. He seemed to know he was where he belonged.

With our new family of four on the road again, we headed over to my mother-in-law's house so Matt's family could meet Carlosse. On the way, we heard a little voice pipe up from the back seat with a question, instantly addressing Matt as Dad. Matt was astonished at the instant acceptance and the young child's intuition that Matt was his new father.

A little later, we rang the doorbell with two kids in tow. Matt's mom opened the door with a sparkle of joy in her eyes. Matt's dad and his wife were also there, along with Matt's brother and sister-in-law. Carlosse was having a warm welcome, for sure.

Stepping into the foyer, I peeked to the left and saw that the kitchen table had wrapped packages waiting for Carlosse. We steered him, slightly shy and bewildered from the attention, into the kitchen and set him on a chair at the table, by the presents. What a wonderful distraction and way to break the ice with our little man!

Sweetly and quietly, he opened his gifts. Grandma Anita had bought him a Spider-Man plate, cup, and silverware, and Grandpa Rich and Grandma Sheela had purchased him a Spider-Man car and figurine. Now, in Spider-Man heaven, he was less overwhelmed with the attention.

Interacting with Carlosse about the toys, Grandpa Rich got him to answer some questions, but otherwise, Carlosse was quiet in this newfound life.

"He is adorable. I just want to hug and kiss him," Grandpa said.

"I know exactly what you mean," I answered.

"He is so sweet and beautiful," Grandma Sheela said.

"He is. He is incredibly sweet," I replied.

Chatting with Matt's family as Carlosse played, Matt's mom commented on how lucky we were to be able to offer him the love and care he deserved. "He's a little waif, and I love him!" she laughed. I agreed. His clothes were clean but way too big, and he was in desperate need of a haircut. He was a little ragamuffin, and he was ours.

The warm welcome from Matt's family in Spokane and from my family afar was comforting. We had heard stories of families not accepting adoption, but that was not our story. My mom practically crawled through the phone, she was so excited about Carlosse, declaring her need to meet him as soon as possible. Matt's family bought necessities, toys, and clothes and were present for our now frequent visits and birthdays. They relished their new roles as grandparents, aunts, and uncles. Adoption had spread from the two of us to all the people we loved. Our new addition, Carlosse, had deepened the bonds of family once again, drawing us closer than we had ever been before. Everyone was eager to love this new child, to love this new nephew and grandson, to love this little boy. Our hearts were full to bursting, overflowing, brimming, and cram-packed with adoration. We had added another child to our family. We had added another stretch mark on our hearts.

7.

Foster Care

After Carlosse had been with us for two months, I received a phone call asking us to foster a six-year-old boy. His current placement was not working out, and he needed to be moved ASAP. *Really?* I thought. In one year, we had gone from zero to two kids and now they were calling about another child to foster?

This phone call wasn't even about adoption. They were requesting a foster care placement (temporary care of children in our home), a shift for us. So far, we had been pursuing only foster-to-adopt, not even entertaining the idea of foster care. What about Carlosse? He was brand-new to our home. Unfortunately, I had no vacation or maternity leave left because I had used it all for Alex, so Carlosse had immediately gone to daycare. We were still bonding, still figuring life out, and just getting into a routine, and they wanted us to add another child?

I informed the social worker that although we technically had room for one more, we had just gotten our son from Spokane and I didn't know how the Spokane social worker would feel about us adding another kid so soon, so, effectively, no. Plus, I was already stretched by a three-year-old who was walking and talking. A six-year-old? That was even older and way out of my wheelhouse. Finally, I needed to talk to my husband about it. We always, always had to be on the same page regarding adoption and foster care, and if someone said no, the answer was no, and right at that moment, my answer was no.

Hanging up the phone, I felt a little troubled. Was it guilt I wrestled with? I didn't think so. Well, maybe a little bit, but it was more that knowing-in-your-gut troubled. There is a difference. What if we were supposed to take this six-year-old to foster? I stopped in my tracks for just a moment, closed my eyes, and prayed. "Lord, if we are supposed to have this little boy be a part of our family for a time, then have the social worker call back. If she calls back, I know we are supposed to say yes." Later, when Matt got home and I shared my thoughts, he agreed; this placement was out of our hands.

The next day, I got a call at work. It was the social worker from the day before. "Hi, Niki, I called Spokane to talk to your social worker up there, and she saw no problem at all for you to take this six-year-old boy."

Pausing, then laughing, I shook my head. Not that she could see me, but I still shook my head. This social worker had gone above and beyond the call of duty, tracking down Carlosse's worker in Spokane in hopes of finding a home for this young man. God was obviously greater than my "no," and for the sake of this child, I was grateful that the workings of a higher power were truly higher than mine.

"Yes," I said, drawing out my answer.

"Yes?"

"Yes, we will take him. I prayed yesterday that if we were supposed to have him in our home, you would call back, and here you are calling me back. My husband and I have already talked, and we are both in agreement."

Within a couple of hours, our household of four had grown to a household of five. We had all boys now. Even our darling dog, CJ, was a boy. I was sorely outnumbered and we were full to capacity. Alex was sleeping in his room, and Carlosse and our new foster son would be sharing a room with a bunk bed, right across the hall from Alex.

As we visited for a few minutes with our social worker while our new addition surveyed his surroundings, the social worker mentioned offhandedly that our foster son had a little sister about Alex's age, at another foster home in town. As I watched the young boy explore our home, I wondered what it would be like to be separated from a sibling. I have a brother. Would I have been okay as a child if he hadn't been living with me? No. No, I would not have been. Our new foster son did have visits with his sister, but what was that compared to being around someone you love for twenty-four hours a day every day? I knew that DSHS worked hard to keep siblings together but sometimes there just weren't enough foster homes available to keep them together—again, the situation simply was what it was. There wasn't a home in Pullman licensed to keep them together. Even we couldn't keep them together because of the size of our house. All our bedrooms were full.

Tucking all three boys into bed that night, I contemplated how our life had changed so rapidly. We had gone from childless to a family of four, and now we were officially foster parents for this little boy, all in less than a year. When we had first considered foster care, I truly hadn't even known what it was. Growing up in a small town in Alaska, I had never heard of such a thing (although I am sure it existed). We had stumbled upon foster care through friends, and now there we were, fostering one kid and adopting two out of foster care. Now we were not only adopting through DSHS but were also fostering. We had realized that jumping into a new and unknown area of life could present journeys we might never have considered traveling on, and foster care was that journey for us. Both of our hearts had grown, changed, expanded, and stretched during a year, and it was good. Our hearts were big enough now to consider and accept a foster child. We were now ready to do something we had not been ready to do before.

With our home completely full, we began to think about moving to a bigger house—not just because we had two kids and a foster son, but also because our foster son had a sister he wasn't living with, and maybe we could do something about that. We couldn't even think about reuniting these siblings until we had room to support them. If we bought a bigger house with more bedrooms, we could get licensed for more kids. We would also need a minivan; our one car wasn't going to cut it. The back seat of our Subaru Outback was full of three car seats that were tricky to buckle in, though I was becoming quite proficient.

With both of us working full time and figuring out how to parent three very different boys, the days were flying by. Within six months of our foster son's placement, we offered on a bigger house, purchased a minivan, and moved a little closer to town. We took on sister, and boy, was that ever a change!

This little girl was eighteen months old and had the brightest, most beautiful smile, white-blonde hair, and a penchant for hollering if she wasn't being held. Her former foster mom had simply strapped her on her back and carried her everywhere, but that wasn't going to work with me because I worked full-time. This little girl and I were going to have to figure out a new way of living.

Every morning, we had four kids to get ready for the day, which included eating breakfast, making lunches, and me mentally planning dinner. Then, every morning and evening, Matt and I had three separate daycares and a school to drop off and pick up at. We were stretched to the limit, but the kids were together. We could do this.

One morning at work, a co-worker came up to me and said, "Niki, it just dawned on me that every single morning, you have to get these kids up and ready and out the door to four different places around town and get here by eight a.m. I just never thought of all you had to do before." I smiled at her and thought how nice it was for someone, anyone, to notice.

I quickly checked myself, however. God had noticed. Sometimes my kids noticed. I had four kids in my house who were on the receiving end of every hug, kiss, holler, breakfast, lunch, dinner, bath, and mommy meltdown. Whether they acknowledged it or even knew the depth of our sacrifice, it was happening. God saw, our children saw, and we saw. *That was enough*, I told myself, though I will admit that having a little outside encouragement bolstered my strength and validated my calling.

Because our circle of friends and community hadn't had much exposure to foster care, we often found ourselves educating. I heard some...interesting things from well-meaning but ignorant people.

One of them was "I mean, foster care is kind of like glorified babysitting, right?"

"No, actually, it's nothing like that," I replied. "These kids have come from major abuse, neglect, and trauma. They aren't flippantly removed from their homes. Some kids in foster care have PTSD comparable to some veterans. You do not traditionally parent these kids. So, no, it's not glorified babysitting. It's intense therapy."

Another was "You get paid though, right?"

Sure, if you want to call forty-six cents an hour being paid and totally and completely laying your life down every single second of every single day. The correct term is "reimbursed," because if you are a good foster parent, you take care of the kids in your home and you buy them new shoes and new clothes, send them to camp (if financially possible), feed them good food, and do for them everything you would do for your own children. So technically, you usually end up paying to be a foster parent.

Another common question was "How do you give them back? I could never do that."

Actually, though, you can. You can give them back if you make it about the kids. They aren't yours in the first place. The goal of foster care is reunification. Your heart being broken from getting attached, compared to the love you pour into the child's broken heart...well, there really isn't a comparison. You will cry when they leave, but you won't regret loving. I'm convinced our hearts have an endless capacity to love, because love is an action, a choice. You will be okay for loving and letting go. They won't be okay if we don't step up and love them.

For eighteen months, we had the sibling group placed with us. Their birth mom tried to get better. She went to rehab, and things were looking good, but when someone comes out of rehab and the only place that person has to go to is back to the circle of friends and family who fed their addiction, chances for success are slim.

Unfortunately, this mom was not successful. Matt and I often talked about her circumstances. "What if we could transplant this family to another state, in a healthy circle of friends, and give them daily support?" I wondered. "This family would make it. I know they would." I do believe that the very best place for children is with their biological families, but only if it's safe and in the best interest of the children.

Relatives traveled from the east coast to meet the kids and to seek out possible adoption, but sometimes adoption with a relative doesn't work out. Sometimes, whatever is going on in the birth family means it's not safe for the relatives to care for the children, and they, in the best interests of their family, say no. It can be more complicated than you think. Looking in from the outside, it's easy to pass judgment on these families tangled up in foster care, but over the years, we have found ourselves growing in empathy for birth families—not for all of them, mind you, but some of them. Once we learned their stories, it was harder to judge too harshly. Often, these parents had spent time in foster care themselves. They had been abused, neglected, and molested. Most of these birth families love their children, believe it or not, but they are broken and, in turn, have broken their children. It's not right, and it does not excuse neglect and abuse, but knowing their history can maybe help us hold these families with compassion. When we hold others with compassion, we aren't saying the behavior is okay. We are saying, "I see you. I see what you have been through. How can I help you?" Thinking about our six children and their birth families, there are some in their birth family I have held with compassion, knowing their love for my children. Then, there are some I have not. There is pure evil in the world, and evil is evil and has no place in our home.

When the time came for relinquishment of parental rights for the two foster kids in our home, Matt and I were faced with a choice of whether to adopt. The logical answer would be for us to simply keep and adopt these kids. After all, they had been with us for almost eighteen months. In fact, it almost seemed heartless to say no to adopting them, but in foster care and adoption, you try to do your best to make decisions based on what you know is right for you and for the kids. That is the best you can do. You may not know the impact of that choice until years down the road, and that is, simply put, part of being a foster parent. Hindsight is truly 20/20.

We had grown from zero to four kids in a year and were stretched beyond stretched. Besides hosting a monthly foster care support group in our home, we were parenting-traumatized kids. We needed a break—badly. Recently, we had connected with a couple in our church who had been foster parents in a neighboring state and were getting licensed in Washington. They wanted to adopt. The mother, after meeting our foster kids, looked at me and said, "These are our kids. I just know it." Then I explained to her that relinquishment of parental rights was under way and there was a good chance that the sibling group we had would be coming up for adoption. Soon, we began to see each other at church services, lunches, and at their house. The kids had an overnight and began to build relationship. That summer, when we went on vacation, our foster son and daughter stayed behind for a two-week visit with this family. Our foster kids had gone on all previous vacations with us, so it was hard leaving them behind, but we were working on a possible transition to a permanent adoptive home, and when parental rights were relinquished, we wanted them to be as ready as possible. We knew we wouldn't have the final say on where the kids would go for adoption, but we could help lay the groundwork with a family who wanted them for keeps.

When we finally got the call that parental rights had been relinquished, it was sobering. Our foster son was old enough to understand where his life was headed, although he had held out hope of going home to his birth mother. Many months had passed since he had seen his mother. Visits had been suspended because of multiple no-shows on her part. It was very hard for a young boy to understand why he wasn't seeing his mother anymore.

Once we knew for sure that he and his sister were not going home, it was time to talk to him. We, the foster parents, were going to be the best choice to break the news because we had the most relationship with him, which meant we were the ones who got to sit down and tell him of a loss greater than I could imagine. The moment is vivid and burned in my mind, like it happened yesterday. It's not every day you deliver devastating news to a vulnerable person you love.

Evening had arrived, and our picture windows, overlooking our backyard, were black, reflecting the cozy living room inside. Dinner had been finished for hours, and the younger kids were bedded down in their respective rooms. Soft light glowed from our lamp in the living room, and Matt and I were sitting together on the couch with our almost-eight-year-old foster son. How did one go about telling a boy that he would not be returning to his home? That he would no longer see his mother? The answer: gently and compassionately. Though we had just spent more than eighteen months with this young man and were the best people to break the news, I had a feeling that I would never again want to be in this situation.

"So, you know how you have lived here a long time?" we started.

"Yeah."

"I know it's been hard not seeing your mom. It's been a while, huh?"

"Yeah."

"Well, we have some pretty tough news for you tonight."

Silence.

"You aren't going to be able to go home."

Silence. Truth. Resignation. He had already known in his heart that this news would come eventually. He had known because of the lack of visits, the length of time he had spent in foster care. He had known.

He looked directly into our eyes, unblinking. Those eyes knew too much.

"But, there is a family who loves you so much and wants you to live with them forever. Can you guess who that is?"

"You guys?"

I had known that was coming. Of course we loved him. It was the obvious answer. How could we communicate our love for him but also say no?

See how complicated foster care is? I knew that by saying no, in some ways, we were saying, "We love you, but not enough to keep you permanently." We were going to be another piece of rejection in his life. But we had also communicated clearly from the beginning that we were only his foster parents, his temporary home.

"We do love you so much," I told him. "But there is another family that, the second they laid eyes on you, knew that you were supposed to be their kids forever. Do you know who that is?"

With eyes visibly lighting up and a smile gracing his little face, he blurted out the name of the family he and his sister had been spending time with.

"Yes. That's exactly who wants to adopt you and make you their son, and your sister their daughter."

He nodded slowly as he let the news sink in: He wasn't going home, and he wasn't staying with us permanently, but he was going to be adopted by another family. He seemed to accept the rather large bombshell. He and his sister would stay together.

We would still see each other at church and outside of church. They were going to a family that wanted them forever. Huge change was coming, but maybe change he could wrap his mind around, in time.

The next month was a whirlwind of activity as we worked on adoptive placement. The kids did more overnights. I started having the little girl call me Mama Niki instead of Mama. Her brother had called me Niki from the beginning, but she was having some difficulty understanding what was going on. We spent time having dinner and playing in their soon-to-be-new family's pool. We worked on transitioning relationship and worked on letting go.

Eventually, the day came to transfer their case over, and then they were gone. The quiet in our house was palpable. We had worked hard on making the transition as easy as possible for brother and sister, but we were left reeling at the gaping hole in our household. Carlosse, just shy of five, struggled to understand where his brother and sister had gone. From the beginning, both Alex and Carlosse had known that this foster care placement would most likely not be permanent, and our foster son had even called Matt and I by our given names, but reality set in, and my heart broke as I watched Carlosse grieve over the loss of his siblings. We hadn't fully understood the impact that fostering would have on our children. Matt and I grieved too, but we were also relieved to be focused on our two boys and to see the kids we had fostered find permanency. I call what Matt and I were experiencing *relief grief.* The burden and work of four children in our home had been lifted, and two kids had found their forever family, but we had to let go. It was a beautiful thing. It was a hard thing. It was the right thing.

The day after our foster kids had moved to their new family, during church service, brother and sister got up with their new family, and the family announced that they were adopting the children and excitedly introduced them as their own. I stood in the sanctuary at the back of the church with tears streaming down my face. Those kids had been my kids for more than a year and a half.

A friend saw me and walked over. She held my hand and smiled compassionately at me. No words were needed. Even though I knew that we weren't called to adopt these kids, that they were exactly where they needed to be, I still grieved. I grieved and worked on letting go, knowing my heart would eventually be ready to do it all over again. The next day, Matt and I communicated with DSHS that we needed a three-month hiatus to rest. I just needed a little time. A little time for my heart to heal. A little time to catch my breath, and a little time to say good-bye.

8.

The Third Bedroom

During our three-month break as foster parents, big change was in the air for us as a family. After he had worked for ten years as a lab manager at Washington State University, I encouraged Matt to dust off a dream he had set on the shelf in 1994: becoming a genetic counselor. After watching his unhappiness year after year in a job he had no passion for, I thought it was worth it for him to at least pursue his options while our family was still young.

We knew it would mean graduate school, but we weren't sure what that would look like for our family. Matt was also aware of my dream of writing, and before we moved forward with any more thoughts of graduate school, he started a conversation. "What about your dream, Niki?"

"What about my dream?"

"Your dream of writing. My dream isn't more important than yours. I will put graduate school on hold if you feel strongly about pursuing your writing."

The respect Matt showed me in that moment meant everything to me, but I knew that it wasn't my time. We had two small boys at home and were working on building our family. Him going to school now, while the kids were young, made the most sense. The sacrifices we would be required to make for him to go back to graduate school seemed more practical with a young family. Besides, I could write anywhere, any time.

We began to put things in motion. First, Matt would need to find out if he had the necessary experience and credentials to even apply for a genetic counseling program. Becoming a genetic counselor was extremely competitive—only about 10 percent of applicants to such programs are accepted. He had picked up a couple of minors over the years after receiving his bachelor degree in biology with an emphasis in genetics: one in psychology and one in molecular biology. We knew he had the correct undergraduate degree to apply for graduate school, but did he have the right life experience? His resume was bolstered by his coauthoring of several published research articles, and then he discovered that his years as a foster parent counted as crisis-counseling experience, which was required to apply. This meant the only requirements left for him to fulfill before applying to graduate school were scoring well on the Graduate Record Exam (GRE) and job-shadowing a genetic counselor.

With our information gathered, the path looked clear to move on to the first step of application, taking the GRE. Matt began the rigorous schedule of studying for the test. Purchasing a study guide, he got to work. This was before the Internet was ubiquitous, so he studied with books.

After exceeding his expected score on his GRE, he drove to Walla Walla and Spokane, Washington, to job-shadow a genetic counselor. Next, because we were a family of four, he researched programs with good financial aid. After narrowing down his choices, he applied to seven programs. I encouraged him to apply to every school he wanted to go to. This was his one shot. We had the money in savings, and regardless of whether he made it in to graduate school, the money would be well spent as he pursued his dream. Application fees, plane tickets, and hotels were not cheap, but dreams never are.

All seven programs wanted to interview him. One of the schools interested in him was in Texas. He hadn't initially even known of the school in Texas, but a program director of a graduate school in Minnesota had encouraged Matt to apply to a Texas school because the state had oil money, meaning tuition was cheap. The Texas school responded to his application with an invitation to interview, but Matt brushed off the interview for financial reasons: Traveling to seven schools to interview would cost a lot of money. He said, "I don't want to go to Houston, Texas. It's hot down there. This is a lot of time off work. This is expensive."

I replied, "They offered you an invitation. They see something in you. You never know what door is going to open. You have to at least give it a shot." After all, this was a school he had heard of through another program director and had applied to on a whim. They wanted to talk to him, so why not knock on that door? I knew he was tired of travel, but, he could add Texas to his final trip for interviews. It would be foolish, in my opinion, to not explore all his options.

He finally agreed and set up the interview. His last trip would include an interview in North Carolina, South Carolina, and Texas, all within a week. It would be intense.

Interviewing in South Carolina after Texas, Matt told the assistant program director there that he would never go to Texas because it was just too hot. Despite the heat, though, Matt had been impressed with the school. The University of Texas (UT) at Houston is the home of MD Anderson Cancer Center, which is one the most prestigious cancer facilities in the world. UT Houston is also located in the largest medical complex in the world, which employs more than 100,000 people. On top of that, the UT Genetic Counseling program reported that 93 percent of its graduates passed the National Board Exam on their first try.

After all the interviews were concluded, we waited. Matt had his schools ranked from one to seven, and Texas was number seven. When match day—when all the schools made their offers—arrived, he did not get offers for the top two schools on his list, but he received three other offers and was wait-listed at two other schools. UT offered him a scholarship over the phone, which moved UT from number seven to number one on his list. At that moment, he remembered what he had said to the South Carolina assistant program director: "I will never go to Texas."

He had no idea that the assistant program director from South Carolina was being promoted to program director at UT–Houston. Boy, did he eat those words! Sometimes what we don't want to do is exactly what we need to do—and sometimes the places we think we don't want to be are exactly where we are supposed to be.

Matt officially accepted UT's offer, and finally, after all the time, effort, and money, we knew where we were headed.

As Matt had been traveling, interviewing, and eventually receiving offers for graduate school, we continued to be foster parents, mostly doing respite care (respite care is temporary care of children, usually providing relief for their usual caregivers). Sometimes we had a placement for a weekend or for up to five days, and sometimes overnight or for just a few hours. The arrangement was perfect for us during this busy time. After Matt was accepted and we knew we would be moving to Texas, our social worker knew about our upcoming life change and called to place children based on our future move.

Then, out of the blue, I got a call at work. (I think I always got a call at work.) "Hi, Niki. We are calling to see if you could take a placement for a thirteen-year-old girl. We know you and Matt are moving in July, but this girl, she has been kicked out of every foster home she has been in. We know you will only have her for a few months, but would you consider taking her?"

This was a big decision, for sure. We were in the process of uprooting from our home of ten years, and they wanted us to take in a blossoming teenager. Well, I said what I always said. "Let me talk to Matt. Because we're moving soon, we have a lot on our plate. I need to talk to him, and then I will call you back."

Hanging up the phone, I knew we had room for the girl. Plus, there was an ending date for the placement: the day we would be driving out of town. Maybe we could help this young girl.

Matt agreed that we should at least try. It was a little daunting to know that not a single foster home had been a good fit so far, but we were a young family, so perhaps a younger foster mom and foster dad with young kids would be just what she needed. Besides, we knew some of her case history, that she was prone to lying. Knowing that, we could accept her and trust that when the right opportunities arose to help her, we could. A wise foster mom told me once that if a child was doing something wrong, that something was a character issue, and maybe you didn't catch the child in the act the first time, but that was okay, because the "something" would come up again, and when it did, we could address the issue. What this young lady needed was stability, love, a schedule, and a family. We said yes.

Adding a girl to our all-boy house was interesting. She was bossy, beautiful, lost, confused, and in survival mode. We immediately included her in the mix of our family and our schedule. We knew our time was short, and we did what we could while we could. She lied, and we loved. Our foster daughter had her own room and space, and her school was only a few blocks away. I went to counseling with her weekly and took pictures for her memory book. She traveled to Oregon with us for a Memorial Day weekend getaway, and as trust grew between us, we got to help her, and she helped us. She helped us see that we were capable of more than we thought we could handle. We worked as a whole family, and it wasn't long before our foster daughter melded into the Tschirgi mold.

During this time, Matt and I traveled down to Texas for a weekend to find an apartment to rent. Our two boys stayed with friends, and our foster daughter stayed with another foster family she knew from our church. I was introduced to Houston over the whirlwind weekend. We had some big decisions to make. Matt would not be working or would be working only part time, and I was going to be a stay-at-home mom, so we were going to be living very frugally, buying only the necessities for the next two years as we survived off student loans—loans that would eventually have to be paid back. Our biggest decision was whether to rent a two-bedroom or three-bedroom apartment. We needed only two bedrooms, but that would close the door on foster care, and possibly on our current foster daughter, as we weren't sure of where her case was headed, though we both agreed that if we were allowed, we would take her to Texas with us for adoption. We also knew that if that didn't work out, we could possibly get licensed as foster parents in Texas.

We went back and forth over what to do and had several lengthy discussions. Money said, "Get two bedrooms," but our hearts told us to go with three. Because of our uncertain future regarding children, it seemed that we needed the three bedrooms, even though it would cost us money we didn't have. But dreams and callings do cost. They will always cost.

We signed a lease for a three-bedroom apartment about seven miles from the Houston Medical Center in Pearland, Texas, and I had a visual on our new life. I had seen not only the city and Matt's school but also our new home. With that, we headed back to Washington state.

As the time drew near for us to move and I organized a giant garage sale to sell as much as possible, including one of our cars, reality began to set in. We were selling everything, uprooting from all we knew, and taking a giant leap of faith. We were settled in Pullman, and we were deeply involved in our fostering community. But we were leaving.

There was a lot to be done to move out of state, and we shifted into overdrive. Besides both Matt and I wrapping up our jobs, we had a house to list and get ready to sell, as well as movers to pay. We were depleting all our resources to invest in this dream, but we were taking a calculated risk.

In addition to uprooting, we were in talks with our social worker regarding our foster daughter and her future. Her relatives were moving to the Pullman area (ironically, from Texas) to help with our foster daughter and her brother and sister, who were in another foster home, so it looked like she would be staying in Pullman to be with extended family. After we received this news, the foster family from our church that she had stayed with for the weekend we had been in Texas stepped in and asked for her case to be transferred to them after we moved. This meant she would be going to a family she knew and would be staying in the same church community and school system. It was the best we could do for her, since the decision was out of our hands.

Before we knew it, we had reached the evening before our departure. This would be our foster daughter's last night with us. Tucking her into her bed—which was now just a mattress on the floor—I sat with her. I had no idea what to say, and I decided that being present was going to have to be enough. As we sat together, I looked around the room. Everything she had arrived with, along with everything we had purchased for her, was packed and lined up against the wall. Earlier, I had printed off every picture I had taken of her for the brief months she had been with us and placed them in a photo book. I know it wasn't her whole life, but it was part of her life, and I wasn't going to move away without leaving her with some semblance of history.

The next day, our foster daughter left to be with her new foster family.

Our 1:30 p.m. appointment for the movers to arrive came and went. Some friends came to help us in our hour of need. Four hours later, the movers pulled up next to the house. By this time, we should have already been mostly packed and perhaps even gone.

The movers ambled over to us to check in and then had the gall to request packing our things the next day because of their late arrival. They also hadn't brought *any* packing materials—which we had arranged and paid for—for our breakables.

"Our paid contract states that you are to move us today," Matt told them calmly. "We are heading out of town tonight to move to Texas. We need you to pack us up tonight."

"Well, if we are going to pack tonight, we need to eat dinner first," they pushed.

We had just ordered pizza, so Matt invited them to share dinner, but they said that wouldn't do.

We felt backed into a corner, and one of our friends, Dan Akins, really stepped in and helped us. He offered to pick up Chinese food for them. This seemed to placate them, but to us, it felt like a ransom payment: "Feed us, or none of your things will be packed."

Dan then ran to Kinko's five minutes before they closed that night and bought several hundred dollars' worth of packing materials, which we happily expensed back to the moving company.

Not a great way to start our move across the nation, obviously. It was a hellish day, but our friends rose to the challenge and did our movers' job for them, helping pack our breakables and load the moving truck. We were expected in Spokane that night for the first leg of our journey, and as the hour grew late, the boxes and some of the furniture still hadn't been loaded, so some faithful friends, including Dan Akins and Lily Sherman, stayed to make sure the job was done...and done right.

With our minivan packed to the hilt, our family slowly pulled away from our house as the sun set over the rolling Palouse hills. We were leaving a mostly empty house that hadn't yet sold, all our dearest friends in Pullman, and our tight-knit fostering community. We were leaving our foster daughter. We were leaving all that we knew, and all that was comfortable. We were leaving home.

Quietly, I rested my forehead against the passenger window, watching the last vestiges of light leave the day. Soon, complete darkness surrounded me. All was silent in the van—a sure sign of exhaustion—as the kids slept and Matt and I were left to our individual thoughts. I knew this was right, but it felt strange. Even though we hadn't had a smooth departure, I remembered how faithful God had been as Matt had studied diligently for the GRE, how He had shone a light on the path to Texas, and His astonishing provision for school with a scholarship. What we were doing was right, no matter how I felt about it at the moment. I knew that feelings lie; the proof was there before me, and I held on to every confirmed step we had taken. I held on to every instance I knew to be true, and I let go of all that I knew was not. We were going to Texas for at least the next two years, and somewhere in Texas was someone meant for our third bedroom. We just didn't know who.

Arriving in Houston on August 3, 2006, for graduate school, we had no way of knowing that Zack, our son, was being born that *very day* in the very same hospital that Matt would do clinical rotations in. Seventeen months later, near the end of our stay in Houston, we would find out exactly why our hearts had told us to spend the money we didn't have on that third bedroom.

9.

Zack

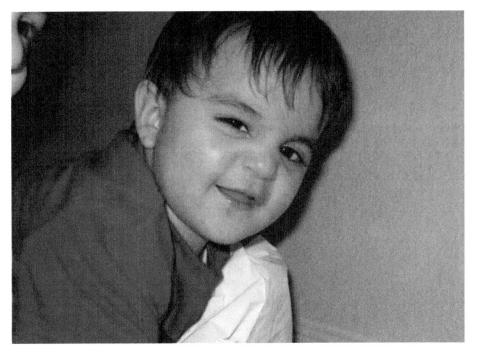

Zack's first day at our apartment in Pearland, Texas.

E xiting the movie theater in Denver, Colorado, where we were vacationing to visit my brother and his family, I felt my phone vibrate in my purse. Frantically digging for it as usual—it had a wonderful knack for sinking to the bottom or losing itself in an inside pocket—my fingers finally found the evasive object. Quickly retrieving it from my shamefully stereotypical black hole of a purse, I answered. "Hello, this is Niki."

"Hi, Niki! This is so-and-so with Depelchin Children's Center. We have a wonderful match for you for foster care!"

Shaking my head incredulously, I told her that was wonderful but we were currently out of the state of Texas on Christmas vacation in Colorado and wouldn't be back for another ten days.

"Oh, that is perfectly fine. You see, Zack, who is sixteen and a half months old, needs to be moved from his current foster home, because that home is closing. It is fine that you won't be back for a bit; you can just come pick him up when you get home."

Seriously, the social workers have a solution for any answer other than "yes." Most social workers are quite talented, sacrificial, underpaid, overworked, and woefully underappreciated.

Listening to her describe this little Hispanic boy, I couldn't help but feel he was truly a perfect match. Our agency knew that we were most likely moving in June, following Matt's graduation, and Zack needed a placement for only three to four months. We would therefore be a great transition home for him before he was moved back to his birth family.

"Can you give me a few more details about Zack?" I asked.

"Sure, he is a sweet little guy but hasn't yet learned how to walk. He is crawling, though. He was born five weeks early." My mind wandered somewhat as she talked more in-depth about Zack's background. We had finally gotten our Texas foster care license almost two months prior, and several placements had fallen through, which was odd in a city that was desperate for foster parents. In Washington, we had gotten calls all the time to foster, even while our house had been full, but there we sat in Houston with no placement that had stuck. We had said yes to several children, but at the last minute, they had gone to other foster homes, or shelters had stepped in, or they had returned to their biological homes. Then there had been silence. Not one call in a city of millions. Not one call…until Zack.

I reflected on this and knew that our home had been held open for him. I was especially certain of that fact after the social worker informed me that Zack was a good eater and slept through the night. One of our main concerns about taking a baby at that time was Matt's rigorous school schedule and the absolute necessity of him getting a good night's sleep.

Snapping back to attention, I refocused on the social worker and told her that Zack did sound like the perfect fit, particularly because he was foster-care-only for the next few months and we would most likely be moving. Plus, as a stay-at-home mom, I had more flexibility during the day than a lot of people to get Zack scheduled for the services he needed. I knew that Early Childhood Intervention (ECI) would do wonders for him learning to walk.

Matt agreed, and we said yes to Zack.

Our time in Denver passed quickly, and before we knew it, we were headed back to Texas for the start of Matt's final semester in graduate school. We both knew that this last semester would be intense with thesis work and that I would be the primary foster parent at home. We set up and planned a routine so the kids and our soon-to-be-new foster son would see daddy every day. Him leaving at six o'clock every morning to catch his van pool before anyone was up would mean that his only time with the kids during the weekdays was from dinner to bedtime. Having dinner as a family would therefore become an even higher priority than usual. After we put the kids to bed, Matt would study until ten o'clock. This would be our routine for the final push through his last demanding semester.

Arriving back in Texas just after the new year, we got back in contact with our agency to set up a time to pick up Zack. Settling on a Saturday morning transition, we focused on getting Zack's room ready. We were glad we had buckled down financially and gotten the three-bedroom apartment. Here, at the end of our stay in Houston, Zack was proof that the decision for the extra bedroom had been correct.

With a crib in place and new pajamas folded neatly on Zack's mattress, we were as ready as we were going to be. Going from two to three kids was going to be a change. Of course, we had done it before, but not in a different state and with my husband in graduate school!

Dropping our kids off at a friend's house, we made our way to our agency. In Texas, the state contracts out to private agencies, which was new to us. In Washington, we had worked directly with Child Protective Services; in fact, we were licensed through them and always had direct contact with CPS. Not so in Texas. Our social workers, class instruction, home studies, interviews, etc. were all done through a private agency.

Often, people who are interested in adoption ask me, "How do you pick an agency?" or "How do you decide what route to choose for adoption?" or even "What made you decide on foster care?" There is no formula or simple answer for those seeking to adopt. My recommendation is to always do your research and knock on doors, and you will know in your heart which agency is right for you. CPS regularly holds an orientation that is free of charge and lets you gather information about what it means to be a foster parent, or to foster-to-adopt through your state. If possible, I encourage those seeking to adopt or foster to attend an adoption conference or event. Often, there will be multiple agencies set up to talk to you about domestic or foreign adoption. Plus, there are sessions you can attend to learn more about the process. I clearly remember that once, when Matt and I were sitting in on a session about overseas adoption, by the end of the talk, we looked at each other and shook our heads, knowing it was not the path for us. I'm sure others sat in that same session knowing that Guatemala or wherever was where their journey was headed.

During the summer between Matt's first and second years of graduate school, we looked into becoming licensed foster parents in Texas. To our delight, our forty hours of PRIDE (Pre-Service and Adoptive Parent Training) from Washington would transfer to Texas. Matt's schedule did not allow him to do forty hours of training to become licensed in Texas, but it did allow him to do the eight additional hours required by Texas. The door for us to become licensed foster parents in Texas flew open, and we walked right through.

We had chosen our agency in Houston after Matt had attended a one-day adoption event. Taking precious time out of his studies on a Saturday, he had visited all the booths, gathered the information on all the agencies, and talked with everyone he could. He had come home saying he felt strongly that Depelchin was our best fit. Looking through the information that he asked me to review, I too felt that this was the agency we were supposed to go with. No one can tell you what you are supposed to do. You simply keep stepping and steering, remembering that you cannot steer a parked car; you have got to press the gas pedal. The answers come as you move forward, just as they came for us in Houston.

After arriving at Depelchin in the late morning, we were ushered into a homey, warm, naturally lit waiting room. I knew this moment would be emotional for Zack's current foster family; we, too, had transitioned foster children out of our home. Tears were inevitable. I knew the foster family adored Zack and that if they could have kept him, they would have. There was no doubt in my mind that Zack was loved in his current home. As we sat quietly—and anxiously, I might add—Zack's foster mom and foster sister finally arrived with Zack in their embrace.

Zack's head swiveled our way. As he stared silently at us with his large, Hershey-bar brown eyes, I could tell he was taking in the scene as his foster mom and sister quietly cried while handing him over to me. He had to sense their grief. He arched his neck back to get a better look at me, and our eyes connected. I watched his little mind working to figure out what was going on as he gently and soundlessly rested in my arms. I imagined it was difficult for him at seventeen months old to grasp the situation. He had just left the arms of the only mom he had known and, unbeknownst to me, had just been transferred to the arms of his forever-mom-to-be.

After sharing a few private words with Zack's foster mom and sister, Matt picked up Zack's belongings, allowing time for a few more good-bye kisses. Promising to keep in touch, cradling Zack in my arms, I headed out to our van with Matt. We had purchased a lovely, softly padded navy blue car seat for Zack, and as he nestled into his new surroundings, he quietly continued to stare. He stared at me. He stared at Matt. He did not make a peep. Again, I marveled at his eyes. The eyes truly are the windows to your soul. How many times had I seen his eyes in other foster children in our home? Carlosse had had those eyes when he first came to live with us: lost, hurting, sorrowful, and deeply wounded. Driving away from the only family that Zack knew, we headed back home to settle in for the afternoon with our new foster son.

After we arrived home from picking up Carlosse and Alex, we set Zack on the floor to see what he would do. Matt and I both observed his cherub face and commented on how we could see the gears turning in his head as he looked at us, attempting to figure out this new twist in his life. Even today, we can still see those gears turn in his eleven-year-old brain.

Carlosse and Alex joined Zack on the floor as he tentatively scooched around on his hands and knees. His eyes alight with curiosity, he made his way around the small apartment, examining the furniture and his new space and home. I made a mental note to call ECI first thing Monday morning, then scooped up our new little guy for his afternoon nap. Would he go down okay? Would he cry? Smothering his face and hair with kisses in hopes of loving the sorrow away, I opened the door to the third bedroom, which we had rented in faith. As I laid him gently down in his crib, his large, luminous, lost eyes gazed up at me. Immediately, he shoved his hand into his mouth and began slurping on his ring and middle fingers, comforting himself in a way I could not. I pulled the blanket up around his chin and brushed his wavy brown hair back from his forehead. His eyes followed my every movement. I said, "Nigh-nigh," and shut the door. Maybe this wasn't going to be a difficult transition after all.

He seemed like a good napper. In the tick-tock of a few hours, my heart had already been lost. It ached again with that familiar ache—not of sorrow but of growth. In only a few moments' time, Zack had added another stretch mark to my heart.

10.

There's Your Sign

Alex, Zack, and Carlosse in Pearland, Texas.

Finding our routine with Little Z, as we affectionately began to call Zack, happened quickly. While the older boys were at school, Z and I got to know each other. We practiced drinking with a straw and faithfully had in-home therapy twice a week. He did not want to walk, so the therapist suggested I buy a child-size toy walker and have him give it a go. The walker did the trick. With something to hold on to, Z was soon moving around the apartment with ease and we watched him bloom before our very eyes. With his legs working properly, his words, which had been few before, began to form and come out of his mouth. Amazingly, in three short months, he went from not walking to running as a toddler should, and from barely talking to babbling coherent words. He was also eating us out of house and home. He was such a messy eater that we had to buy a tarp to put under his chair. (Truth be told, not much has changed since then!) The loneliness and sadness gradually dissipated from his eyes. Z was healing in our home.

During this time, Matt was sending off job applications around the country and had been invited to interview in Alabama. Knowing that you can't just take a child in foster care out of state, we reached out to our social worker to get the proper paperwork for interstate travel. We were not going to leave Z behind after he'd had so much change in his life. Some people might ask, "Why such a commitment to a child in foster care?" Because for however long we had him, he was our child. Simple as that. Where we went, he went. The other two were old enough and secure enough to stay with friends. Z, however, was not.

I traveled with Matt to meet with a realtor, and I took Z along. It was his first time on a plane and his first time out of Texas.

Upon returning from Alabama, we received a phone call about Z's case. "We have set up a final visit for Zack and his siblings with their birth mom before she relinquishes her parental rights," the social worker told us.

I paused for a moment before commenting, "Heartbreaking."

"I know, but we knew this was where the case was headed. Zack and his brother Tommy—who is three—are supposed to move soon to be with relatives here in Texas."

"Okay, we will be there. Of course we will be there."

We had known that the original plan was for Zack and Tommy (who was in a different foster home) to each go to an aunt in southern Texas after relinquishment. Matt and I have always been for reunification if possible and if it was in the child's or children's best interest. I knew the judge wasn't overly excited about splitting up the boys, but at least they would be in the same city together with relatives and would see each other, right? That thought did little to comfort me, though. Was the situation ideal? No, of course not. Was the separation even right? Absolutely not. What would be right was for them to never have been in foster care in the first place and for them to be growing and thriving in their biological home in a healthy, loving, and safe family. But these children had been born into abuse and neglect, and this was the best the state could do. It made me angry. The boys deserved to be together.

My eyes focused on Zack across the room as he played with his toys. I was confused. This little boy had easily found a place in my heart, and in a few short months—maybe even weeks or days—I would need to say good-bye. I wasn't ready, but I needed to be. I knew we could give him a stable two-parent home with his brother. I wrestled with the judge's decision and questioned my own beliefs about family being best. Hadn't I always said kids needed to go home or to family if it was safe and good? But there I was, waffling about Zack leaving us to live with his single aunt, away from all his siblings. Maybe family wasn't always best. In this case, siblings were being placed in different homes, and there was nothing I could do about it, so I resigned myself to the court's decision with a heavy heart for these kids.

A few days later, I packed up our Little Z and made my way into the heart of Houston for his final visit with his birth mom. Showing up at the office, I had no idea what to expect. I sat down in the waiting room across from other family members who had arrived to support Zack's birth mom. As Zack and, later, Tommy, were ushered back in to a meeting room by social workers, I caught the only glimpse I have ever had of my children's birth mom. She walked past a window and made her way down a hall. She was a stranger to me, but she would be a very important stranger in the months to come, though I didn't know it.

Zack and Tommy's older brother and sister, who were together in another foster home in North Houston, were already back in the room for the visit. I hadn't met them yet and had only just found out about them—and that no relatives had stepped forward to request the older kids. I wondered about their future in their current foster home and how it made them feel that no relatives wanted them. Sitting in the waiting room, across from other family members, who eyed me cautiously, I wondered about the awkwardness of the moment. Was I the enemy in their eyes?

Eventually, Zack returned to the waiting room with a social worker, who placed him back into my waiting arms. As I cuddled and interacted with him, one of the women sitting across from me watched me closely.

"Are you Zack's aunt?" I asked her.

"Yes," she said.

"Would you like to hold him?"

"Yes…thank you."

Hesitantly, I handed Zack over to his aunt and immediately knew it was the right thing to do. How would I feel if that were my niece or nephew in the arms of a stranger? I'm sure she hadn't seen him in months, perhaps a year.

Cooing sweet words in his ear and kissing his face, she absorbed her time with him as I sat quietly looking on. Unfolding before my eyes was a strange and foreign scene. There was no freedom for her to see him whenever she wanted. For almost two years now, he had been in the custody of the state of Texas, and still, there were many unknowns. Although the court had ordered Zack and Tommy to eventually move in with two separate aunts, it hadn't happened yet. On top of that, this wasn't even the aunt who would be taking Zack home, but there she sat, loving on her nephew in a sterile government waiting room.

With the visit winding down, Zack's aunt reluctantly but stoically placed him back in my arms. "Thank you," was all she said, but the look in her eyes said so much more. She was so grateful I had allowed her to hold, cuddle, and love Zack. She knew I didn't have to share Zack.

I was glad that I had. "You're welcome," I told her.

Zack's birth mom didn't come out while I was in the waiting room. After I had slipped Zack's jacket on him, he and I made our way out to our van, and I buckled him into his car seat. Watching him suck on his fingers, I knew that he had no clue what had just happened. He was not even two years old and had just lost his mother. Gone. That would be the last time he would see her for a long time, maybe forever. His life had permanently changed.

As Zack looked at me with his trusting brown eyes, I laid a wisp of a kiss on his forehead, pulled myself into the driver's seat, and headed back home, troubled by the brokenness I had seen that day. I have never seen Zack's birth mom again.

February rolled around, and I began making plans with Zack's Court Appointed Special Advocate (CASA) worker for a sibling visit to see Tommy and his two older siblings, Liza and Luis. Tommy was still in a different foster home than Liza and Luis, putting the four kids in three homes. I was grateful to know that Liza and Luis had been able to stay together, but I was dismayed once again at this prime example of the great need for more foster parents, especially ones who could take in whole families. Originally, Zack and Tommy had been placed together, but issues in their first placement had caused both children to be moved. They had been unable to stay together, so with them spread apart, we did the best we could, and that was to arrange visits. With Zack and Tommy's looming move to be with their respective aunts, who lived hundreds of miles away, in South Texas, it was imperative that we reunite them soon.

March arrived quickly, and toward the middle of the month, we found out that yes, Zack would be moving to be with his aunt. Thankfully, we had a sibling visit in place at Zuma, a fun center in North Houston, but Tommy would be unable to attend. Arriving with Zack securely on my hip and with my other two boys in tow, I scanned Zuma for a familiar face. Our CASA worker would be there with the older kids, who I had not yet met. I finally spotted the worker at a long table, sitting in front of a blue birthday cake, which she had brought to celebrate Liza's March birthday. I shifted my eyes around the table, and they landed on a middle school-aged Hispanic boy with thick, spiky hair who was sitting quietly at the table. *That must be Luis.* My eyes crinkled in laughter as I imagined the amount of product he had clearly used to get his hair to stand so straight and proud. Next, my eyes then locked on a lovely Hispanic girl with intricate braids in her hair. *She is so pretty*, I thought. She gave me a hesitant smile, and I glimpsed braces adorning her teeth.

Quickly, I approached and sat down with Zack. I could tell that Liza and Luis were delighted. This was why I had come—so Liza and Luis could spend time with their little brother. Seeing them together solidified in my heart what I already knew needed to happen: sibling visits as often as we could do them.

After our time at the Zuma Fun Center with arcade games, pizza, and go-carts, our CASA worker and I planned on getting another visit in motion. A month later, we were all together again at the Houston Zoo. Taking pictures and spending time together was good but sad. Brief moments of relationship and making a scrapbook for memories isn't the same as living life together. Plus, Tommy wasn't there, either. The only time I had seen Tommy, other than at the final visit with the children's birth mother, was at a city-wide picnic for foster families and their foster kids, where I had spotted him playing in a sand box and had covertly taken a picture of him.

Not long after our zoo visit, we discovered that Tommy had moved to South Texas to be with his aunt, though Zack stayed put in our home. We waited and wondered about what would happen to this little boy in our care. Why hadn't he moved too? The answer came a few weeks later. The aunt who was supposed to take Zack had apparently fallen off the face of the earth. The judge was furious. He had reluctantly agreed to have the boys separated and go to family, on the knowledge that they would be in the same city and with relatives. He was known for ruling in favor of siblings going to non-relatives instead of being separated and had been under a lot of pressure at the time of his decision for Zack and Tommy to rule in favor of birth families. Now, one brother was hundreds of miles away from all his siblings. Zack's placement with relatives was falling apart.

I could see the writing on the wall: The door to adoption was squeaking open. Matt and I had a decision to make about Zack. Would we adopt him? Although my answer was a resounding yes, my husband was up to his eyeballs in thesis work and was terribly unsure of what to do.

Lying around in our living room that next weekend, I broached the subject to Matt. "So, what do you think about adopting Zack?" I asked.

My husband was silent for a long moment while formulating his answer. I could see him thinking as he lay quietly on the couch, Zack playing inches away on the carpet.

"It's not that I don't want to. I just don't know. I've been in graduate school this whole time, with hardly any time spent with him."

"You know, if we ask to adopt Zack, he has a brother out there too. Tommy. He's down in South Texas. I think if we ask for Zack, we need to ask for Tommy too. We can keep them together."

Matt was quiet again. I knew I was asking to move mountains. We were wrapping up our life in Houston, and I was posing a loaded question in asking if we could grow our family by two more kids. Matt didn't have an official job offer yet and wasn't sure about Zack, and I was throwing Tommy into the mix.

As we chatted on about Zack, our little boy toddled out of the living room and into Carlosse and Alex's bedroom, where most of the toys, games, and books were. Soon, he was toddling back out on his chubby little legs, heading straight toward Matt with a book in his hands.

Oh, how sweet, I thought. *He wants Daddy to read to him. That's a first.*

Approaching Matt with sure and steady steps, Zack lifted the book and literally tossed it on Matt's lap.

As Matt picked up the book, I saw his eyebrows raise high on his forehead. An incredulous laugh escaped his lips. "Look at what Zack brought me!" he said in wonder as he held up the book.

Leaning forward, I read the title of the book. Out of the dozens of books on the boys' bookshelf, twenty-one-month-old Zack had grabbed and given to Matt, the one who needed convincing, the book titled *Adopted and Loved Forever.* Laughing,

I jumped up off the couch, pointed my finger directly at Matt, and yelled, "There's your sign!".

A few years before, one of my closest girlfriends, Karin Grinzel, had purchased the book for me while she had been visiting Colorado Springs, Colorado. She had known the adoption wait was hard for us, and she'd had a strong impression to bring that book home for me. Little had she known that her simple gift would play such a complex part in the life of not only Zack but also his siblings. Her one act of obedience to God's nudges became a powerful tool in placing the parentless in a family.

What was left to discuss? Matt couldn't say no after that. I e-mailed our social worker that day, officially requesting to adopt both Zack and Tommy. Zack's social worker and CASA worker agreed to write letters to the judge on our behalf, petitioning for us to be Zack and Tommy's adoptive parents.

Our time in Houston was running out. Matt was wrapping up his graduate school work and had secured a job in Dallas, Texas. We would be moving soon. We finally got word that Zack and Tommy would be ours, and we began working on transferring our case to an agency in Dallas, though Tommy was still in South Texas.

Liza had her *quinceañera* at the end of May. I was delighted that her foster parents were throwing her such an amazing cultural party, to celebrate her fifteenth birthday, marking the transition from childhood to young adulthood. At her party on March 24, she was gorgeous. Decked out in a formal teal dress, hair, makeup, and salon-painted nails, she looked like a princess.

Matt and I had never been to anything quite like that night. Food, laughter, dancing, and joy emanated from the warehouse that had been transformed for the event. Friends and family all showed up to celebrate Liza. What a gift she was being given! I was humbled to be included, and Zack was passed around to all his aunties and cousins, who relished every moment with him. It was joyful, but sad because of the broken ties that no longer held them together. Matt and I, along with our CASA worker, were the only white people there, and most of the people attending spoke Spanish, but none of that mattered. We were welcomed with open arms and were encouraged to eat, eat, and eat some more, and to dance. We didn't need to speak the same language to communicate love. While placing a card and a potted flower on Liza's gift table, I attempted to consume the last of my horchata (a milky drink), and we headed home for the night.

Liza and Luis dancing.

Four days later, we received word that our social worker was going to be calling Tommy's aunt to let her know that he was not going to be staying with her and was being adopted with Zack by us. I was torn up inside, though the court had decided that keeping Zack and Tommy together was in the boys' best interest. How would I feel as an aunt to have my nephew taken away? I couldn't fathom it, and I sent an e-mail that day to my mom:

> *Please pray for our social worker today. She has a big day. She needs to call the aunt to tell her that she doesn't get to keep Tommy. It's just so emotional I'm sure. And pray for the aunt too. It's so hard. I feel very caught in the middle.*

We were also working hard to transfer our case to Dallas. That had to happen for us to take the boys to our new home. We could not leave Houston until paperwork was filed. It was the end of May, and we were moving to Dallas on June 14. Would I have to stay at a hotel in Houston or live with friends until the paperwork was done?

Five days later after the social worker called Tommy's aunt, the ball was officially rolling. Our new agency, Hope Cottage, had a copy of our home study to review, and we needed to fill out new paperwork. The agency needed our foster-to-adopt application and our new address to arrange an Environmental Health and Fire Safety inspection once we arrived in Dallas. Prior to us moving, the agency also needed to meet with us and to see our new home before they could complete the transfer, all while Matt was graduating and we were adding Tommy to our home and packing up to move from one large city to the next. Matt agreed to complete the drawing of the floor plan for our new home in Dallas for the agency and, eventually, the walk-through of our new home before I and the kids moved to Dallas. This wasn't our first rodeo. Thankfully, our new home did not have a pool, which could have led to delays in licensing of our home by the agency for safety reasons. I had plenty of outlet covers, fire extinguishers, and smoke alarms on hand. Armed with experience, we were going to make this happen.

Life was a flurry of activity on the last day in May as we filled out new applications for background checks and waited to see if we needed to be fingerprinted again. I threw up my hands at listing our past ten years of residency, so Matt calmly took that sheet from my clenched fingers as I turned away from him to sort through our apartment so the movers could pack us. In a week, Tommy would arrive, and a few days after that, we would be heading up to Dallas to move Matt and to do our pre-move visit with Hope Cottage.

Matt would be starting his job a week before the movers came and before our duplex was available to rent. Thankfully, we had friends in the Dallas area, so Matt had a place to stay while he started his new job. I would be in Houston with four kids—one of them being brand-spanking-new to our home—and moving us by myself up to Dallas

We also needed to request and receive court approval for Zack and Tommy to travel out of state in July, when I would be driving the kids to Wisconsin to visit my family. Because our case moved from Harris County to Dallas County and we were now working with two counties, the whole process could take longer than the recommended two weeks' request for travel. I had completed the Overnight, Respite, and Out of Town forms so the state would have a record of where we would be on our travels to the Midwest. As I listed every hotel, address, and phone number of places we would be staying and how I could be contacted if necessary, I mulled over the fact that this was not normal vacation planning.

I wondered if there was anything left to do before our move. Probably, and it would have to be done at the last minute, and we didn't even have Tommy placed with us yet. Winding down our time in Houston wasn't like a clock stopping with no warning but rather like a fast-moving timer counting backward. There was no pause button or reset or start over. Our move date had been established and our request to adopt Tommy had been approved. We were adopting a child we had never officially met, because his little brother had wiggled right through all our self-defenses and paved the way up to the doorsteps of our life. Zack had left an entry wide open for Tommy to walk through. We just had to wait for him to darken our door and light up our hearts.

11.

Tommy

Tommy the morning after he came to live with us.

June came in like a wild Texas storm as we prepared our home for Tommy, packed up Matt to move to Dallas, discovered we did *not* need to repeat our fingerprinting, tracked down our TB blood test results, obtained copies of birth certificates for us and our children, and located our marriage license buried in a file cabinet. We also gathered proof of health, auto, and renter's insurance so we could officially transfer our case to Dallas for the boys.

Because of Matt's job change and our move to Dallas, we also needed to verify our household income and give an accounting of our debt-to-income ratio to document Matt's ability to support our family. Matt therefore got to work on his end, gathering his first pay stub, a copy of our most recent tax return with W-2, and a revised version of our foster-to-adopt application with a consent to check our credit. Adoption doesn't just happen; it's work. A lot of work.

Our apartment buzzed with activity as we eagerly awaited the arrival of our newest son. Our social worker, who had flown down to South Texas to pick him up, would be bringing him. The clock on the wall kept ticking away the minutes later and later. Finally, around nine thirty that night, the social worker showed up with almost-four-year-old Tommy in hand, a small suitcase trailing behind him. Our worker looked travel-weary, and she quietly relayed to us that at one point, she had thought she would not be returning with Tommy, because nobody had been home when she had arrived to pick him up. Tommy had eventually been located, however, and here they were. Exhausted, the social worker left our apartment.

Tommy had not been at any sibling visits with us, so this was our first official meeting. Immediately, he began to explore. He opened every single door, window, and cupboard. Matt and I exchanged looks as he opened the door to the outside and stepped out: That night, we would be dead-bolting the door for sure. Next, taking Tommy by the hand, we showed him his toddler bed with a new comforter neatly displayed, and a new pair of pajamas folded, waiting just for him. Zack was already fast asleep in his crib. Tommy peered in curiously at the new room and the little brother he didn't know, then went about exploring once again.

While he was busy discovering his new home, I picked up his suitcase and opened it to see what possessions he had. My heart sank. The tiny suitcase held only a few items of clothing, one size too small, for the winter season, even though it was June in Texas. He had nothing. No toys, no stuffed animal, no clothes that fit. Glancing up at our new busy toddler, I was grateful that he at least had pajamas for the night. I would have to do some shopping the next day, for sure.

Corralling in this new busy boy, Matt and I managed to get him in his pajamas, brush his teeth, and tuck him in to bed. Quietly, I left the door cracked, and I watched pensively as he drifted off to sleep, wary that he might wander out—not just out the bedroom door, but also out the front door.

The next few days were a blur as we got Tommy as comfortable as he could get before a move, and then we and the four kids hit the road to drop Matt off in Dallas, Matt in the new car he had purchased and me in the minivan. We had a lot to get done in our new city on that Saturday afternoon, as Sunday afternoon would include our big pre-move interview with Hope Cottage, as well as the walk-through of the new home we were renting.

On the way out of Houston, we stopped at Old McDonald's Farm so Matt could be part of a sibling visit with Liza, Luis, Tommy, and Zack. It would be the first time the four siblings had all been together in almost two years. We waited a little anxiously at the entrance until Liza and Luis were dropped off by their foster mom. The kids immediately reunited and began to play all together, including Carlosse and Alex. Finding a large pile of sand, the boys began climbing to the top, sliding down, burying each other, and riding a metal dump truck to the bottom. Liza even participated, getting herself dirty while playing with her brothers. All eight of us picked pumpkins and had snacks. Nearing the end of our visit, as I stood close to Liza near the pumpkin patch and a leafy pecan tree, a gentle whisper touched my heart.

What if these kids come up for adoption?

I stilled. What if they did? What if Liza and Luis did not stay in their current foster home to be adopted? Calmly and peacefully, I tucked the thought of adopting the older kids in to my heart and felt my heart expand. I felt my heart stretch as if to get ready to make more room. I didn't say a word to Matt about what I had felt that day, but I knew I would be ready if, or when, the call came.

I looped my arm through Liza's, and we wrapped up our visit with a picture of all the kids, then drove the older kids back to their foster home. After saying good-bye and promising to visit soon, we finally made our way up to Dallas for our jam-packed weekend.

We arrived in Dallas late Saturday afternoon and spent the evening relaxing, knowing that Sunday would be a full day. On Sunday, we first spent several hours at Hope Cottage as we completed our pre-move interview. Matt was given a questionnaire to answer about our huge life change, to submit before I would move up with the boys the following week. After our walk-through with the agency at the duplex we were renting, Matt planted his laptop on the floor of our empty future home and got to work on his questionnaire. I took the kids for a walk to Carlosse and Alex's future elementary school, which was a block away, so Matt could work quietly and quickly. I would have a long drive back to Houston the next day, and exploring our new neighborhood would allow me to check off the final box on my to-do list for the weekend while Matt completed his questionnaire.

The kids at Old MacDonald's Farm. Top row: Carlosse, Alex, and Luis.
Bottom row: Tommy, Zack, and Liza.

How do you feel about graduating?

I feel awesome about graduating for a number of reasons. I've wanted to be a genetic counselor for over eighteen years. It is a dream I had in high school. For many reasons, I was not able to pursue it until now. It has been a hard road, but one I'm glad I took. My family has been extremely supportive of me. If I had to do it all over again knowing what I know now, I would do it again.

How do you feel about the move and the new job?

I am very excited to stay in Texas! We moved down here from up north. I've never lived farther than seventy-five miles from where I was raised. I had a lot of apprehension about going to school in Houston. However, I fell in love with Texas after living here a few months. I really wanted to stay in the state. I'm so fortunate that a position opened in Dallas. We wanted to stay in Houston, but Dallas looks like a great place to raise a family. We want to stay here and have our roots go down deep. We've moved twice in the last two years. I want this to be a place where our children graduate from high school.

How do you feel about adopting a sibling set?

Niki and I have debated between having two or four children. I was raised with two brothers. I know that having three kids means it's always two against one. When Zack came up for adoption, I honestly felt better about adopting him and Tommy, instead of just Zack alone. I believe siblings should be together, if possible. Zack is totally a part of our family, and I'm sure with time, Tommy will be too. I know it will be a huge change for everyone involved. We've never adopted someone this old before. I believe with some love and boundaries, Tommy will do well.

Are you aware of what hours you will be working?

My hours are pretty much 8:00 a.m. to 5:00 p.m. I don't have to travel much, maybe one or two conferences a year. There will be a couple of days a month that will be at-home work days, where I don't see patients and work on paperwork.

The questionnaire was the last piece of information our agency needed. With its completion, our whole life was laid bare and we could officially move the kids to Dallas. Now, all that we had left to do was move.

Slipping behind the wheel of our van that evening, I kissed my husband good-bye, double-checked my rearview mirror, made sure I had all four kids accounted for, backed out of the driveway where Matt was standing and waving good-bye, and headed back to Houston…alone. It was June 9, 2008. Tommy had been with us only a few days, and I was embarking on a solo expedition for this final week. Friends needed to be hugged and said good-bye to, the movers needed to pack up our apartment, and I was going to have one final sibling visit with all the kids.

The highlight of my week without Matt was organizing a visit to the home of Liza, Luis, Zack, and Tommy's other two brothers (seven and nine at the time). They lived with their dad in Corpus Christi, Texas, which was just over three hours southwest of where we were living in Pearland. The drive was easy and brought us right to the beautiful ocean for fun memory-building time with the kids. After stopping at the home of the brothers to load them up in the van, we headed straight for the beach.

"Do you boys like to go to the beach?" I asked.

"Yes! But we hardly ever get to go. Dad works and we don't have a beach pass. You need a beach pass to drive on the beach and park there too."

"Well, today, that's where we are going."

Huge grins threatened to split the faces of the two additional rowdy boys now inhabiting my van. After picking up a beach parking pass at the local store in Port Aransas, Texas, I drove right onto the sand, unloaded the kids, and let them loose. Tearing off and kicking up sand, the two Corpus brothers headed straight into the waves with their clothes on, with Zack toddling behind after them. Nonstop playing in the sand and sun ensued for hours as the kids built sand castles and buried each other from the waist down.

Later, plopped down on my beach towel, with Zack napping in my lap, I considered all their futures. In two days' time, I would be taking two of the siblings away to a new home, away from their siblings in Corpus and Houston. Separated. The challenges lying before us were of a steep order. Corpus was around eight hours away from Dallas, so sibling visits once or twice a year were doable but not easy with a husband beginning a new job and four small children at home.

"Niki! Niki! Look!"

Giggling and the shout of my name drew my attention back, as the kids buried Liza even deeper in the sand. The sun was starting to swing low, signaling that it was getting near time to go. Reluctantly, I gathered up all the sand toys, fishnets, towels, and kids. Racing to the outdoor showers on the beach, all eight of them began the arduous task of rinsing off. The kids being buried in the sand guaranteed that not all the sand would relinquish itself, no matter how long they stood under the quiet cascade of water, but it didn't matter to me. Memories were what counted. Sand could be vacuumed out of my vehicle. A long time ago, I had surrendered to the fact that my van would see sand, leaves, dirt, and whatever else my kids left behind. My vehicle wasn't more important than fun.

Driving back to the brothers' house in Corpus Christi, I was pleased at the ease with which the kids bantered back and forth. The time and distance that had separated them had evaporated swiftly. Before foster care, these biological siblings had all lived in the same tumultuous, neglectful environment with their birth mom, moving from city to city. Immediately after Zack's birth, all six kids had been removed and placed in foster care. Moving from one relative to the next over the course of two months, the kids had finally been split up, two by two, to different foster homes. Eventually and miraculously, the two brothers in Corpus Christi (who are the middle two brothers between Luis and Tommy) had been reunited with their dad by a social worker. The social worker had turned over every stone to find him, finally happening upon an old neighbor at a former address who had pointed her straight to him. His boys had disappeared with their mom, and he hadn't known where they were, or that they were in foster care. While the two boys had settled back home in Corpus Christi with their dad, the other four children had remained in non-relative care in Houston. Despite the changes and their months apart, the kids had found common ground easily today.

"Niki, can you be our mom?" one of the boys asked.

How do you answer a question like that? "Boys, you are exactly where you are supposed to be. You are with your dad, who loves you so much."

"I know, I know, I know. But it would be great to have a mom."

Pulling in to the narrow driveway later, I turned off the van and watched them all clamber out.

"Liza, look at me!" shouted one of the Corpus brothers.

Hanging from the tree in the yard, Luis let out a whoop, and soon, all the boys followed suit. They were climbing, hanging, and swinging like wild monkeys on branches. Laughing, Liza went to join them, and I got out my camera to take a few pictures for memories.

The boys' dad came out to greet me. "*Mija*, did you have fun?" he asked me, using the Spanish word for "daughter."

"Yes. Yes, we did," I told him.

We stood in companionable silence, watching the kids play in the yard. I still had a three-hour drive home to my apartment—count it five hours if I was going to drop off Liza and Luis in North Houston. I knew our time had to come to a close and it was time to say good-bye. I headed back to the van to gather up the boys' stuff from the beach, reaching through the window to grab the beach parking pass off my dashboard. It was good for the year, and I didn't know when I would be down again. It might not be for another year. Turning to the boys' dad, I handed him the beach pass. "Here, you take this. Take your boys to the beach and have some family time. Go fishing. I know from Luis how much you love to fish." I knew they didn't have much. I also knew he was doing the best he could for his boys.

Wetness flashed in his eyes as he took the parking pass and tucked it in his pocket. "Thank you, *Mija*."

Nodding at him and smiling, I began the herculean effort of rounding up my bunch, and then we gave our last good-bye hugs and loaded up the van for our trip home. As we began winding our way back to the freeway, I looked into the rearview mirror and saw the two brothers jumping and waving wildly at us. It had been a good day.

It had also been a tough day, with the joy of reunion and the sorrow of separation all within hours of each other. Again, it was what it was, and within the parameters we had been given, we had given our best.

Unfortunately, our best never seemed enough. As I dropped the oldest kids off, I wondered when we would see them again. Would we travel down for Thanksgiving, or maybe spring break? I didn't know.

Moving day was upon us, and boy, was I grateful that Matt's new job had provided a moving package as part of his offer. The movers packed up our belongings, loaded them on the big truck, and drove everything away...no Chinese food required. I simply needed to buckle four kids in to car seats and drive.

The first few days in Dallas were almost unbearable, however. For some reason that escapes me now, we did not get our furniture until three days later. I had four children under the age of seven, one of them I barely knew, but no dishes, toys, beds, couches, or chairs. Nothing. I lost my ever-loving mind. If it hadn't been for Matt's help in the evenings, I would have gotten in my van by myself and never stopped driving.

Finally, as I teetered on the cusp of complete and utter mother meltdown into desolation and absolute tyranny, our furniture arrived. Things improved drastically. The children had beds to nap on, toys to occupy themselves with, and a kitchen table to consume food at. I had pots and pans to cook with, a bed to sleep in...sometimes...and a couch to *maybe* sit on. Life was looking up.

Transplanted once again to a new city, and with two relatively new kids, we began the process of once again growing roots—to anchor us, to nourish us, and to give us stability and further growth.

12.

Summertime Sojourns

During the latter part of June, my days were full of setting up our new duplex and establishing our children with local doctors. Psychological evaluations, regular checkups, dental appointments, ECI, speech therapy, and occupational therapy: these services needed to be located and scheduled.

July rolled around, and in my infinite wisdom, I drove four children by myself to Wisconsin from Texas. With Matt's new job, he was unable to join us. I had learned many things over the years following adoption on my solo trips across numerous states when Matt had been unable to travel with me. The first of these was to not, under any circumstance, eat in a restaurant. Ever. You must do drive-thru. Corralling six children to stand in line to order, wait for your order, fill your drinks, go to the bathroom, and sit nicely, patiently, and politely at a table is, quite simply, impossible. They won't behave. They have just sat in a van for hours and hours. They are hungry, and they are thirsty...for blood. Eat out of the back of your van at a rest area if the kids need to get out of the car. It doesn't matter that you are alone and no one is there to help you; your kids shoot out of the van like a rocket and roll in the grass while you set up a picnic. Trust me, it works out. Second, have dollar bills at every gas station so said children can buy treats. It's not worth it to say no a thousand times. Not when you are driving alone. You have no reinforcements. Third, purchase numerous new movies or cartoon series to watch during the endless hours of van travel—better yet, rent from Red Box. There is a Red Box on every corner in America. It is worth your money. Fourth, if you do not have something to drink to hand back to your child or children, your life will feel like it is over. You may not think that, but it's true. A child whining for something to drink while you are driving eighty miles per hour through cornfields with no exit in sight will try you beyond what you can handle. Besides, when you stop to get said child a drink, when every child is under the age of seven, they all must unbuckle, get out of the van, and go with you wherever you go to purchase the drink. Just buy a case of water or three boxes of Capri Suns, and call it good. Fifth, be prepared to haul all your children into the bathroom at every gas station with you. You must do this because gas stations are known for unsavory people. Don't worry, you will most likely never again see any of the people who are gawking at you as you herd your children into the bathroom stall. Sixth, always get a hotel with a continental breakfast and pool. By the end of a day in the car, kids need to stretch, shriek, splash, and swim out everything that needs to be let loose. We became adept at clearing the hotel pool. I always felt bad, but what was I to do? It was me, only me. Breakfast was all they could eat and put in their pockets; snack time, after all, was only moments after we left the hotel. I knew how my children worked: Boredom equaled hunger. Finally, give every child a backpack with toiletries, swimsuit, pajamas, and the next day's clothes that they can carry all by themselves. I refuse to haul five suitcases to our hotel room. I did that once, and I never did it again. The lessons were plentiful, the memories well worth it.

Wisconsin was refreshing as the kids spent time with their Grandma, great-grandparents, great-aunties, great-uncles, and second cousins. The family meeting Tommy and Zack was the main point of the trip, but of course we all benefited from the long afternoons at the local pool and the ice cream stops, picnics, dinners, hikes, river swims, and water parks.

Matt and I hoped we could visit Liza and Luis every other month and make a twice-yearly trip to Corpus Christi to see the middle brothers. It was an ambitious plan, and maybe not even possible. After my long trip with the kids back to Texas from Wisconsin, Matt and I worked on getting Liza and Luis up for a summer sibling visit. With the CASA worker in Houston no longer on the case because we had moved, however, finding transport proved difficult. Originally, the CASA worker in Houston had thought she could drive the kids to us, but child-advocate laws said no. We were stuck. There was no one both available and willing to drive them. If the kids were going to get together, we would be the ones to make it happen, which meant a trip down to Houston.

At the same time, we were working on officially having Tommy and Zack placed for adoption. We had finished our home visits and fire inspection and had sent in our adoption paperwork packet with a plan for sibling visits.

August arrived before I was prepared. School was starting in just a few days for the boys, which meant my ability to travel was coming to an end. I arranged a trip to Houston, working feverishly with Liza and Luis's CASA worker to coordinate a sibling visit. Our plan was to go to Galveston for a day, but because of the communication barrier with the kids' foster family (who spoke only Spanish), word of the visit got lost in translation. Liza and Luis ended up being out of town for most of my time down there, and we found it difficult to set up times to meet, even though they had been the whole reason I had traveled to Houston. Eventually, I ended up working with Liza and Luis's case worker because she could translate, and I finally connected with Liza and Luis's foster family at Chuck E. Cheese for dinner so the kids could see each other for an hour or two before I headed back to Dallas. Luis and Tommy were inseparable, and while the siblings played, the social worker translated for me and their foster mom. I wanted her address and phone number so I could send Liza and Luis pictures of Tommy and Zack, and gradually set into place a communication plan between Liza, Luis, Tommy, and Zack.

After we returned to Dallas, we mailed pictures of Tommy and Zack to Liza and Luis. We also sent pictures of Tommy to our social worker in Dallas to mail to the aunt he had been living with in South Texas.

Summer was over for us now that school was about to resume. Were Matt and I ever going to catch our breaths? Probably not, but maybe our kids could catch theirs.

13.

Liza and Luis

School was upon us before we knew it. Carlosse and Alex were already enrolled in an elementary school one block away from our duplex.

Although Tommy had been with us just a few short months, we knew he was going to need a lot more than a standard Pre-K program could give him. Speech and language struggles, social skills, and sensory issues abounded with our newly acquired son. Our social worker had told us to call Head Start as soon as possible for him because spaces were limited. We got him enrolled by the grace of God, managing to secure him a spot during August, almost unheard of so late in enrollment. Tommy had also gone through a psychological evaluation as a new foster-to-adopt placement and was getting settled in to speech and occupational therapy twice a week after school.

I believe I lived in my van between school drop-off, school pickup, and therapy. We had already transferred Zack's ECI case to Dallas, and his therapy was in full swing. Everybody was now settled in to routine—surprisingly, even me.

One weekday afternoon in late August when all the kids were in school and Zack was down for his afternoon nap, I heard the phone ring.

"Hello?" I answered.

"Hi. Is this Niki?"

"Yes, this is she."

"Hi, Niki, this is so-and-so with the Texas Department of Family and Protective Services. Now, I know you are going to say no—" She paused. "But it's the law, and I need to call and ask you if you and your husband would be willing to take Liza and Luis permanently for adoption. Their current foster placement fell through. Since you already have their two brothers placed with you, we need to call and ask you."

Immediately, my mind took me back to Old MacDonald's Farm in Houston, and I pulled out what I had tucked in to my heart to ponder: *What if these kids come up for adoption?* I suppose the social worker thought I was in shock, but truly, it was the exact opposite. A steady knowing permeated my whole being. I was prepared for this phone call. My heart had been prepared back in June.

"Wait a minute!" I said. "I don't think we are going to say no. In fact, I'm thinking we will say yes. But…can I talk to my husband about it first, please?" I laughed.

"Well, yes. I…well, of course. You can have the weekend." She seemed genuinely surprised by my response. Statistically, I knew that the chance of Liza and Luis being adopted together, or even at all, was slim if we closed the door on their future with us. What would happen to these kids if we said no?

"Great. I will call you back Monday with our final answer," I told her, "but these kids are the siblings of our two boys. I know that as teenagers, their chance of adoption is extremely low. We can give them a home. We can do this."

"Great! We'll talk to you Monday then. Good-bye."

After saying good-bye and hanging up the phone, I sat there for a moment. My heart had been ready for that phone call, but I wasn't so sure about my husband's heart. I had never told him about the thought that had come into my heart at Old MacDonald's Farm, and I was positive that adopting these teenagers was nowhere on my husband's radar. Nowhere near, even. He was still settling in to his first job out of graduate school as a genetic counselor, and our family was still adjusting to the addition of two new sons in the past six months, plus a move to a brand-new city. Now we were being asked to add two teenagers to the mix?

Rapidly, my mind scurried over the practicalities that would need to be addressed. We were living in a three-bedroom duplex. I knew that wasn't big enough. Legally, we had to have space for these kids, but we didn't; all three bedrooms were full. That would mean that we would need to break our lease and find renters. We would need to buy a house in North Dallas that was big enough to fit us all, close to Matt's work, and in our price range, during the off-season of the housing market. If it was meant to be, it would happen. Of course, I was getting way ahead of myself. First, I had better call Matt.

How many times had I made a phone call like this to my husband? Usually it was for a foster care placement. The last time I had called him about adoption had been back in Washington when we had gotten the call for Carlosse, but that time, we had been looking to adopt. This time, they were asking when we weren't looking.

I decided not to drop this bombshell on Matt at work. Instead, I chose to have a face-to-face conversation when he got home, so that's what I did. I let him get home and take a few breaths before I came at him.

"Hey honey, when you have a minute, can we chat in the bedroom?" I asked.

"Sure. What's up?" he asked innocently.

"The state called." I said carefully.

"Okay. About what?" he said cautiously.

"Liza and Luis are coming up for adoption, and they asked us to take them."

Matt was shocked, but not surprised. He was shocked because Liza and Luis had been with their foster parents for more than two years and were settled, and their current foster parents had been considering adoption. He was not surprised, however, because this was how foster care tended to trend: Nothing was a sure thing until papers were signed. Foster parents changed their minds for all kinds of reasons, or relatives showed up from out of nowhere, or birth family disappeared or reappeared. Later, after talking to Liza, we would learn that their foster mom had wanted to adopt them but their foster dad had felt too old, because they had already raised their kids and were grandparents.

"Well, what are their chances of adoption outside of us?" Matt asked me. "Their chances are almost nothing as older kids. We know that. We have their brothers, but we don't have the room."

"I know. I thought of that too. If we are going to do this, God is going to have to move some mountains."

"Then we need to say yes, and we need to get a move on this and those mountains," he replied.

"So, we agree that I will call on Monday and tell the state that we will take the kids?"

"Yes…but before you do, I also feel strongly about talking to Carlosse about his thoughts on adopting the kids. Adopting them will disrupt the birth order in our home."

"That's good. He's old enough now to understand adoption and birth order."

Matt took Carlosse, who was seven at the time, out to lunch at the Shake Shack to have a man-to-man talk. Over burgers, fries, and a delicious shake, Matt told Carlosse about the older kids.

"You've noticed we have been spending more time with Liza and Luis?"

"Yeah."

"What do you think of Liza and Luis?"

"I like them. I especially like Luis. He's funny."

"What would you think if we adopted them?"

Carlosse just looked at Matt, so Matt explained, "The place they were supposed to stay at decided not to adopt them, so we have a chance to adopt them. To give them a home. That means if we adopt them, you won't be the oldest anymore. You are a really good oldest brother, but you are going to have to learn to be a younger brother."

Matt waited as Carlosse thought through what Matt had told him.

"It's more important that they have a home than I stay the oldest brother," Carlosse finally said.

The decision had been made. Out of the mouth of a child had come simple wisdom. We had made a family decision. Matt returned home and filled me in on Carlosse's thoughts.

"Alright, time to get working," I said.

And get working we did. Immediately, I was on the Internet, looking for houses that would fit a family of eight in the North Dallas area with a close commute to Matt's work. There was nothing. Matt called our landlord and explained our situation. Our landlord was extremely accommodating and agreed to help us find someone to sublease. He also clued me in to a local real estate website to look for housing. Searching on that website, which I had never heard of before, I found a house meeting our requirements, with only the price and address listed, and no pictures. That's never a good sign, in my opinion as a house hunter. The house was a five-bedroom, four-bathroom house at the very tippy-top of North Dallas, only fifteen minutes from Matt's office. We did a drive-by and found that it was a lovely two-story house in a cul-de-sac within walking distance to an elementary school and a junior high, and just a short drive from the high school. The house was also only a few minutes from Tommy's Head Start, which I had previously been traveling forty minutes round trip each day.

We contacted our realtor, who arranged a walk-through. The house was for sale by another realtor who had moved and was trying to unload the house. Instantly, after walking through the door, I knew this would be our new home. The house was a bona fide mess from the current resident, but Matt and I had experience looking beyond the clutter and grime to see the functionality of a home. Upstairs were two full bathrooms, four bedrooms, and a large game room with a deck facing the back-yard. All the kids could sleep upstairs and have plenty of bathroom space. Liza and Luis could have their own rooms, and the younger boys could continue sharing, two by two. Downstairs were the master bedroom and bath, laundry room, bonus room, living room, and kitchen. This house would fit a family of eight perfectly. At the end of October and with nothing on the market, we had found our some-thing. We had found our house, not listed on any realty site other than the one given to me by our landlord.

We made an offer in October, but when the inspection was done, some big-ticket items were found necessary—like a new roof and extensive foundation repairs. The seller fixed everything and accepted our offer. We had found our house, a house where we could legally have Liza and Luis come live with us, close to all their new schools, and close to Matt's work. Plus, the first person to come look at our duplex signed a lease that same day. We had gotten out of our lease with no issues. In our minds, these were all green lights to adopt the older kids. We would be moving again sometime in December, which meant so would our kids. Again. But this time, we would be moving for the older kids to find their permanent family. Together, we would do this. Together, we were making our way. And together, we would find our way as a family.

14.

First Visit

November came upon us quickly. We contacted the state about our in-process home purchase and phoned our local agency in Dallas for the next two adoptions. The agency was already working to finalize Zack and Tommy's adoptions after the first of the year. We had to wait six months after Tommy's June arrival before finalizing, even though Zack had been with us more than six months, because we wanted to adopt the boys together. Now we had to do two official home visits in Dallas with Liza and Luis before the older kids could move permanently with us to be placed for adoption. The first visit was scheduled for over Thanksgiving.

Driving out to Dallas Love Field Airport, I was nervous. In less than an hour, Liza and Luis would be at our house, to stay for a few days. What were they thinking as they made their way across the friendly skies? We had spent only a few hours together previously during sibling visits, when the focus hadn't been on getting to know each other but on facilitating relationship between the kids. Now they were flying for the first time on an airplane, with their social worker, to another city to visit their brothers and spend more time with us. I was sure we were going to have some awkward moments.

I could just see it: *Hi, I'm your new mom. Your new white mom. Your new northern, very white mom. Your new mom whom you don't know. At all. In fact, you don't even know that this visit is a pre-placement visit, because the court hasn't officially approved the adoption yet and we aren't allowed to say anything. But besides all of that, and the fact that you, Liza, are practically an adult, welcome!*

Parking our silver minivan, I made my way to the baggage claim to await their arrival. Breathing in deeply, I decided that as a mom, it was my job to welcome my new son and daughter with open arms and to be as personable and as relaxed as possible. I could do that for them. So I did what I do best: I talked. I smiled as I saw them making their way toward baggage claim, made my way to them, chattered my hellos with hugs and pushy offers of help with their bags, and steered them toward the airport exit. I was the queen of small talk, and I visibly saw the kids relax as I took charge of the moment, welcoming them in to my heart at full throttle. They needed that. They deserved it. I was the adult, right?

We said good-bye to their social worker, who turned around and got right back on the next plane, then we loaded up and headed out. After I arrived at our now crowded duplex with the older kids, Matt and I set about getting them situated for the holiday. Giving them a tour of our home and apologizing that they would need to use the living room for their sleeping quarters, we let the kids all get reacquainted with each other since it had been three months since our last visit.

Later that evening, because none of our Texas kids had ever been ice skating, we loaded them all up in our two vehicles and made our way to Galleria Dallas, which had an indoor ice rink smack-dab in the middle of the multilevel mall. Liza took to it easily, having been on roller blades before, but Luis hung on to the rink wall as he made his way tentatively around and around. Matt and I each had two kids hanging off our arms. It was exhausting. It was eye-opening. It was wonderful.

Thanksgiving dinner had us packed around our kitchen table, with limited elbow room. Turkey and all the fixings were served along with pumpkin pie. The family did life like we always did, wanting Liza and Luis to get a feel for what it would be like to be a part of the Tschirgi family. From the beginning, Matt and I had decided that as foster and adoptive parents, we would focus our energy on making memories and being a family unit. Vacations, family dinners, local outings, school functions, swimming, and church were top priorities to bring as much "normal" into the lives of our kids as possible. For however long they were a part of our family, they would be a part of every aspect of our family. We weren't going to be leaving any of them behind for family functions if we could help it.

That weekend, we also drove Liza and Luis nonchalantly past the new house and their new schools. We couldn't go inside, but at least we could give them a visual of their new surroundings—even though they didn't *know* these were going to be their new surroundings. We also took them to the Dallas Zoo, knowing that activities were important to lessen the awkwardness and to build shared memories.

The next day was full of commotion as we packed up the older kids to fly back to Houston. It felt strange to say good-bye, knowing that they were our future children. But I took comfort that they would be back up to visit again the week before Christmas for the final home visit. This gave me a measure of peace. The plan was unfolding for them to finish up their semester of school in Houston, then move to Dallas to start their second semester of school. The court just needed to approve it, and then they would have a nice clean start to their new life.

Matt and I had been around this mountain. We had waited for our children before. We would simply wait again.

15.

Second Visit

Our first unofficial family photo.

The week before Christmas was extremely busy. Since Liza and Luis's visit in November, we had officially bought the house and were attempting to get it in order. Hiring local movers, we took a weekend to exit our duplex, deposit everything at our new home, and clean up the mess we had left behind. Liza and Luis's social worker was driving them up from Houston for their second visit in the first week of Christmas break, and I would be driving them back down afterward. We were also set to fly to Washington on Christmas Eve with our four boys. Only some of Matt's family had traveled to Houston for Matt's graduation and met Zack, so we had some introductions to make. Nobody had met Tommy yet.

By this time, the court had approved the adoptive placement of Liza and Luis and the teenagers had been notified—unfortunately, not in the best way. Because Liza's foster parents didn't speak or read English, Liza had opened the letter from the state to read to her foster mom and had found out that she and Luis were being placed for adoption with us in Dallas. She was very angry that no one had told her about the adoption, and she was confused about why we hadn't told them when they had visited over Thanksgiving. This led to a conference call with an interpreter for the foster mom so we could address the misunderstanding.

Emotions settled down, especially after we reassured Liza how difficult it had been for us to keep silent because we had been so excited about adding them to our family. Matt and I had wanted badly to tell her, but we hadn't wanted to jeopardize the adoption process by disobeying a court order. After we explained to Liza about the court order to stay silent, she finally understood that our hands had been tied, and her anger ebbed away.

The days flew by as we did life together in Dallas with all six kids, and on the night before I drove the older kids back to Houston, I sat down with Liza. At the time, I had no idea what she and Luis thought about us and about moving permanently to Dallas. I wasn't even sure that they had much say in whether they came to live with us, but I broached the subject with our soon-to-be oldest child as if she did have a say.

"So, what do you think? Do you want to come live with us?" I asked.

"Well, first you have two of our brothers. But," she said, pausing, "also, you want us."

Looking deep into Liza's shuttered brown eyes, I could see the hurt flash briefly there, then dissipate. Here was a young woman who had voiced over the past couple of days, with bravery and nonchalance, that obviously, her birth mother did not want them. Not only did her birth mother not want them, but neither did any of their birth family. When all the kids had come up for adoption, everybody had wanted Tommy and Zack, the little kids, but no one had stepped forward for the teens. But we were. We were stepping forward, and we didn't have to. We could give them a home, we could keep a family together, and, most importantly of all, we wanted them.

Leaning forward to give her a quick hug, I reiterated what she had said. "Yes, we want you."

After round-tripping it to Houston to drop off Liza and Luis, I returned home exhausted, from both the drive and the emotional deposit I had just made with our children. To top it off, the Northwest had a record-breaking snowstorm in Seattle that shut down the airport for three days, effectively canceling our trip home to see family. The loss of the trip was bittersweet. We had planned the trip long before we had known about the older kids or the fact that we would be moving to a new house. Staying home gave us much-needed time to unpack. Though we were sad to not go, we made plans to travel to Washington with everyone during the summer. In the end, though we were delayed by six months, we would *all* go to Spokane for a summertime visit.

Tying up all the loose ends for our move and new adoptive home study, the social worker asked us for official names for our new kids. Matt and I had talked about this and had spent time and prayer on middle names for them. We just weren't sure if the kids were ready to take on the name Tschirgi. When you have had your last name for your whole life, did you want to change it? I didn't know, so I called Liza.

"Hi, Liza! We can't wait to see you again soon! I have a few questions for you and Luis, if you have time."

"Sure!"

"The social worker is almost done with the adoptive placement paperwork and needs to put down official names for you and Luis. We would like to give you both middles names since you don't have them. Are you okay with Ann Marie? That is my mom's middle name and Matt's mom's middle name."

"Yes. Yes, I like that."

"We picked Joshua Isaac for Luis because Joshua means 'God has rescued' and Isaac means 'laughter.'"

"Just a minute."

I could hear the rustle of the phone as Liza checked with Luis on his two new middle names.

"He's good with that," she said a minute later.

"So…we also need to put down a last name. Do you want to be a Tschirgi? I know you have had your last name, and this is all so new, and regardless what you choose, you are our kids. We don't want you to feel any pressure. You decide what you want."

Liza paused for a moment. I could tell she was deliberating in her mind. Nervously,

I paced around my house with my phone glued to my ear. What was she thinking about these changes? How would I feel if they didn't want to be Tschirgis?

"No, we want to be Tschirgis. We want to be a family. We want us all to be the same name. That's important to us."

Smiling broadly, I told her how great that was and how happy we were. I hadn't realized how much it meant to me to know that they wanted us too.

"Oh, and Luis wants to know if you can change his name from J'Luis to just Luis."

I had wondered about his name, as I had heard only his foster mom call him J'Luis. "Absolutely," I replied. "I will let the social worker know."

"Okay. Good."

Hanging up the phone, I skipped around the house looking for Matt. We were that much closer to finally being united as a family. This was just one more step to all of us being Tschirgis.

16.

A Mother's Right

Monday, January 5, 2009, the day our new son and daughter were supposed to come live with us, should have had me up early with joy. Instead, I awoke with anger and worry. Paperwork had not been completed, and the kids weren't coming as planned. Their new social worker had not gone to their school to officially request their transcripts on Friday, and the pre-placement paperwork that the social worker had sent to us had never arrived. I couldn't do anything about getting transcripts from the school because legally, Matt and I didn't have any authority yet. We were totally dependent on the case worker to take care of these details, but the worker didn't. Two days before they were supposed to arrive, Liza called me, extremely upset.

"Have you heard anything yet?" she asked.

"No. I am so sorry. I have not heard from the worker."

"We were told that we were coming up on Monday. I've already cleaned out my locker and everything at school. My friends gave me gifts and pictures, and I've said my good-byes."

"I don't know why things are such a mess," I told her. "I have two calls in today, and an e-mail trying to get answers. I will let you know as soon as I know anything." As I hung up the phone, the smoldering in my belly roared into a raging inferno. Hadn't my children been through enough? Yes, of course they had.

I sat down hard in front of my computer because I had another e-mail to send. Communication to the new social worker needed to happen on behalf of my torn-apart daughter, and it needed to happen now.

> My daughter is dreading going back to school on Monday. She has no current supplies or class stuff because she thought she was not returning and already threw everything out. She already said good-bye to her friends and teachers. I think she is feeling anxious about having to go back to school and face all her friends and explain everything. She has been super private with school and friends about being in foster care, and this, to her, puts a magnifying glass on the situation. She would really like you to call her. Now. Can you please do

that? I've communicated the best I can with her, but I think it would really help if you called her to answer some of her questions I did not have answers for.

That was all I could do. That, and pray.

Monday came and went, and my daughter's day went much like she had thought it would: terrible. Embarrassing. Friends were confused. She was confused.

"I thought you moved!" they said. And "Why didn't you go?" Even worse was "Why didn't you get adopted?"

I learned that the pre-placement paperwork had been sent to a wrong address, so on that Monday, I acquired and filled out the paperwork, scanned and e-mailed it to where it was supposed to go, followed up on the e-mails to make sure they had been received, and dropped the originals in the mail to the attention of the appropriate person. I wasn't going to be the one holding up my kids' placement. Now, to get my kids home. Because reaching our social worker by phone was near impossible at this point, I took to the computer again to send the social worker another e-mail.

I don't really know what is best at this point (regarding bringing the kids home) except I know I can't fix what is going on right now and the kids are hurting and disappointed. If we can swing it for them to come up here sooner, I'm more than willing to drive down and pick them up. I hope this email doesn't come off too harsh, I'm just trying to over communicate for the sake of these kids and us. I know that Matt and I are their advocates and I'd rather over communicate to try to help them through this process and transition the best that we can. I'm sure it has been a long two years for them, and here they are at the end of their foster care journey, frustrated and confused as to what is going on. This is supposed to be a joyful time for them (they have a permanent home!) but instead it has been full of worry and waiting. Feel free to call me if you have any questions, maybe I'm way off base here. I don't know it all, and maybe I don't have all the facts. I know that we are a team, and I do appreciate the work you do on behalf of these kids and others. I can imagine your workload is large, and we're at the tail end of the holiday season when people have been on vacation. I understand that this causes delays, and know there are things that may have been out of your control. However, what do we do now for these kids? How do we help them now until they can come up here? That's where I'm coming from, and both Matt and I want to be a part of the solution up here. Thanks so much.

In our eight years of foster parenting and adoption, Matt and I had experienced very few hiccups with our social workers. Maybe some of that was because we had fostered in a small community where the case-work load was more manageable. All our social workers up to this point had been angels walking the earth, sacrificing what seemed like everything for the kids in their care, working overtime and spending money out of their own pockets. Maybe this social worker was new or overworked, or maybe just not in the right job. Whatever the case, I could tell that I needed to take some action to push the process along. My kids needed an advocate, and I was going to be an obnoxious one. My scary-mommy hat had come out, and I was wearing it loudly and proudly.

After attempting to get my children's school transcripts for five days, the answer came to me suddenly. I had a court order that said Liza and Luis were to be placed in our home for adoption. That meant legally, I could go get them; it was my mother's right. I didn't have the appropriate paperwork to get their transcripts, but I did have the court order to get my kids...so I did. I decided to drive round-trip to Houston to pick up my kids and bring them home where they belonged. *So what if I didn't have their school records?* I figured that having the kids in Dallas would hurry along resolution to that problem. I called Hope Cottage before I left and informed them that I was going to get my kids. I could feel my case worker's smile through the phone.

Purposefully getting in my van exactly one week after my daughter's upsetting phone call, I made the four-hour-plus trip down to Liza and Luis's foster home in Houston. The smell of pozole (a Mexican soup) greeted me for lunch, and I gladly partook of it with the family. We visited for a couple of hours and, after loading my van with all the kids' earthly possessions, the kids said a tearful good-bye. Then we were off. We were leaving behind their foster family of more than two years, their city, their life, and all that they had known, and we were headed north to absolute and total change. But they would finally be in a permanent family and finally back with two of their biological brothers.

What must that be like? Can you even imagine? Picture yourself at the age of twelve or sixteen, and imagine walking away from your family: your mother, your father, your siblings. Picture getting in to a van with a woman you barely know, driving for more than four hours to a city you don't know, entering a house you visited once, and knowing that for the rest of your life, these people, for better or for worse, will be your family.

Those kinds of deep thoughts swirling in my teenage kids' brains required food, so we stopped off at Sonic and ordered hamburgers, fries, and Coke. The kids quietly and shyly accepted their food and within moments were murmuring their satisfaction. Looking over at Liza and then back at Luis, I asked them, "Haven't you ever had Sonic?" They peered back at me and quietly shook their heads. "Well, good thing we got that out of the way right away!" I had a feeling there were going to be a lot of first times for these new kids of mine.

Satisfied that they were satisfied, I backed out of Sonic and hit the road for the remainder of the long trip back to Dallas. It had been an exhausting day for me, both physically, with all the driving, and emotionally, with receiving the kids and helping them say their good-byes. Back at home, I knew, Matt was preparing our other four kids for the arrival of their siblings. Carlosse, Alex, Tommy, and Zack had made a "Welcome Home" banner for Liza and Luis and had hung it in the living room. I could picture them waiting on the couches even though the hour was getting late.

Pulling in to the cul de sac, I switched off the van and said, "We're here."

Quietly, the kids got out and waited for me to lead them up the sidewalk to the front of our house. Lights from the dining room and stairwell glowed invitingly as I pushed open the door and led our new kids into their new home. Passing through the entryway, I directed them into our living room, where Matt and the four boys were waiting in various stages of wakefulness. Carlosse, our oldest, feigned sleep on the couch because he was so shy. Zack rubbed his groggy toddler eyes, glad that Mama was home. Tommy stared at the newcomers impassively, and Alex circled them like a happy-go-lucky vulture. Matt stood and hugged them both, welcoming them home, and pointed out the banner the kids had made for them.

Soundlessly, Liza and Luis took it all in. I wondered what they were thinking. Over by the fireplace were presents for them that had been sent by family for a belated Christmas. Even though it was late, the kids opened their presents from their new extended family. Luis also opened a wrapped present from us that was a Nerf gun. On the spur of the moment, because our Washington trip had been canceled, and after Luis had gone back to Houston, I had purchased Nerf guns for all the boys as an extra present. I explained to him that the other four boys had the same one and he needed to match them. He stared at it. I had no idea if he liked it or not. He was quiet and looked to Liza for direction. "Thank you," he said.

Later, I found out that the brand-new Nerf gun still in its packaging was the first new toy Luis had ever received. That's why he had stared so hard at the present—he had never had a real, wrapped present before.

"Well, it's late," I announced. "We should probably get you ready for bed, and tomorrow we can unpack. Here, I will show you your rooms."

Liza and Luis followed me upstairs to their bedrooms.

"Luis, this is your room. We can pick paint later for you. I hope what I've done is okay."

Luis just stared once again. I showed him where to put his stuff, and then he followed us to Liza's room, where I said, "Liza, this is your room."

Wide-eyed, the kids took it all in. They would be having their own rooms for the first time. Were they excited? Terrified? Both?

Making sure they knew where the bathrooms and towels were, I left them to get acquainted with their rooms and to get ready for bed. As I went down the stairs, I took comfort in having all six kids sleeping upstairs, hoping Liza and Luis wouldn't feel alone.

The next morning when I went upstairs to check on everyone, the hall light was on and everyone was still asleep. Peeking in on Luis, I saw that he had slept with his room light on. Liza had not, but the hall light was sure to have been a comfort to her in this strange new place.

Later that afternoon, I was putting away laundry in Tommy and Zack's room when Liza hovered in the doorway.

"How are you doing? I asked her.

"I'm doing good," she said. "So, what do I call you?" she asked hesitantly.

Nervously, I looked at this sixteen-year-old girl, practically a woman. "Well, I would love for you to call me Mom and Matt Dad, but I get it. That's hard. You are new here and you don't know me very well, so if you want, you can call me Niki at first."

"Okay. Well, then, I guess I will go back to my room now…Mom."

I could tell the word was foreign and tentative, like she was trying it out on her tongue for size, but I squealed and grabbed her, and hugged her, and I giggled. Like a soppy schoolgirl, I giggled. "You just called me Mom!"

It did take a few weeks for her to work "dad" into her vocabulary, but eventually, she was brave enough to utter the word.

Whatever Liza did, Luis did. Before a month had passed, six kids in our house would be calling us mom and dad. The words were music to our ears.

The Monday after I brought the teenagers home, Christmas break was over. The four younger kids headed back to school, and I took the older kids to school to enroll them, assuming their transcripts had been faxed. Luis's junior high didn't have his transcript yet but took him anyway. Things weren't so easy at the high school, however. Liza had gotten herself all prepared emotionally and physically, only to be turned away at the door because no transcript had been received. I knew in that moment what it meant to see red. I had figured the last thing the state wanted was two kids out of school because of truancy, but apparently, I was wrong. January 21, 2009, was when I finally got both Luis's and Liza's transcripts. Liza enrolled in high school on January 22, 2009, two weeks after I had picked her and Luis up in Houston, seventeen days after their original move date. We put the past behind us, again, and moved forward.

During those first few months of adjustment, I found out what it meant to be a mom of six. My Mothers of Preschoolers (MOPS) group stepped in and brought us dinner for the first two weeks, and was I ever grateful! The laundry, the cooking, the cleaning, the driving...

MOPS had also put out a request for furniture, and people donated everything we needed. Our community rallied and helped during this drastic life change. "How are the kids doing?" people would ask.

"How are *they* doing?" *They* are doing fine," I would laugh. "I just baked cookies with them for the first time in their lives. We are figuring life out. The real question is, how am *I* doing?" I was learning how to cook, clean, and do laundry for eight people, as well as how to run a new schedule of transporting six kids to schools, preschools, therapy, counseling, sports practices, and games. I was exhausted. Matt and I tackled homework together. Every moment of our day was full.

Housework and running the household were things I could do, even though I was tired. Acclimating the kids and getting to our new normal became top priority. The passage of time was what we needed. It was all about the time we had now, not the time we didn't have, or the time we had missed with these kids. They were finally all together, with no fear of separation. I knew how important that was, especially to Liza, who was the "little mother" to them all.

Over the first few weeks, Liza shared with me some of the fears she had felt about her family when they had entered foster care. "When we found out Zack and Tommy were moving to be with our aunts, I was so afraid. I was so afraid I would never see them again. I thought for sure Luis and I would age out of the foster care system. Then I found out that we were coming up for adoption and not staying with our foster family. I was so afraid and so mad. I was so afraid Luis and I would get separated."

There had been so many tears, fears, and emotions already in her short time on this earth. It was nothing new for her to move to a new city, a new school, or a new family. This was what my daughter knew to be normal. She admitted to me that she had already lived a lifetime.

I could see how Liza felt that she had already lived a lifetime, after she had grown up in a difficult home and become a mom to her brother at the age of five. She had been changing Luis's diapers, making his bottles, putting him to sleep at night, and entertaining him day after day when she should have been playing with her toys, putting together puzzles, or tottering around in high-heeled shoes. No young child should have to take on the roles she had. As the years had gone on and more brothers had been born, she had taken on the increasing responsibility of caring for them, and by the time she—at the tender age of thirteen—and her five brothers had gone into foster care, my beautiful daughter had already been doing the work for many years of a full-grown woman. She had even been held back in the seventh grade for missing too many schooldays because her birth mother had kept her home to care for her brothers.

It therefore came as no surprise to me during her early days in our home that Liza had a few adjustments to make. Matt and I had decided straightaway that Liza would not take care of her brothers unless she was paid for babysitting or it was clear that she was helping for a family event. Even then, we would ask, not tell.

"Should I change Zack's diaper?" she asked one day.

"No, I've got it," I said.

Awkwardly, she hung around, watching me take care of her brother. Later, she confessed to feeling surprised and weird because she was used to having that be her role, but then she had felt a tidal wave of relief because she was done: She was done being mom and could now simply be sister.

There were other firsts for her and Luis, too. "You don't mind dealing with us?" she asked one day as we swam at the local pool during their first summer with us.

"What do you mean?" I replied.

"All of us at the pool."

"What? No. I love taking you to the pool," I said. Then I smiled at the lifeguard and, in response to the lifeguard's question, informed her that no, we weren't with a camp and I wasn't the kids' camp counselor; I was their mother and these were all my kids. I guess I could have called it Camp Tschirgi.

"So, we are going to the pool more than once?" Luis chimed in.

"What? Yes! Yes, more than once. I bought a swim pass. Y'all are going to the pool every day. I'm not sitting home with all of you in this heat."

I soon found out that my new kids weren't used to what was normal for our family. They had rarely gone swimming or gone out and done things as a family, and there I was, dragging them all over the city of Dallas to Sonic for happy hour, pools for swim time, the library for checking out books, and the dollar theater for movies. We pulled up to a thrift store one day, and Luis just looked at me as if to ask, "What are we doing here?"

"Don't you want to go to the thrift store? They are so much fun!" I said.

"That's where we always went to get our stuff," he replied.

I could tell he was uncomfortable, and I chastised myself for my insensitivity, reminding myself that my normal was not their normal.

"Sometimes we went to Target with our foster mom because that is where our clothing vouchers were for, but mostly, we went to thrift stores with our birth mom."

"You know what? We'll save this for another day. Let's go to the mall!" I replied.

Liza's eyes grew wide as we parked in the parking garage of Galleria Dallas and entered the huge mall. We beelined for Macy's, where I showed her the clearance section and taught her how to shop the sales. One can never start too young.

"I've never, ever been to Macy's before," she told me.

"*What?!*"

"I've never been shopping in a mall."

I had a hard time wrapping my mind around that. Even growing up in small-town Alaska, I had shopped in a mall. "I can see I have some things I need to do with you," I laughed.

Smiling, she hesitantly perused the racks, and we walked out with a new pair of jeans that I had couponed down to affordable. Having a daughter was going to be so much fun!

Over the next few months, I was reminded often that our way of life was completely bizarre and different to our new son and daughter. All our other adoptions had taken place when the kids had been quite young, and they didn't remember what life was like before us. Adopting older children was a completely different experience. Luis thought it was weird we went on vacation and that we ate dinner together as a family.

Both of them had to adjust to my style of cooking. Luis requested that I make him brown-bag lunches for school even though he could have hot lunch—a brown bag at school meant there was someone at home who cared about him. It was a social-status symbol. That did it for me. I made him his lunch every day after that until he graduated from high school. Often, Luis gave part—or all—of his lunch away, so I learned to pack extra sandwiches for his friends who, like Luis at one time, didn't have someone at home who cared about them.

Soon, we were blending and figuring out life together. Their "adoptive family" blurred to "family." Their status as "brother and sister" changed to "brothers and sister." Life stirred us together until separation was gone and lines were erased. New memories pushed back old, and traditions became essential building blocks that our kids depended on to be nurtured and to grow. At the end of our six-month waiting period, our adoption of Liza and Luis felt more like a formality than anything else. We had already become family.

17.

Congratulations...It's Teenagers!

Top Row: Luis, Liza, Me, Tommy, Zack, and Matt. Bottom row: Alex, Carlosse and our judge in Texas.

ugust 20, 2009. Adoption day. In the adoption community, it can also be known as Gotcha Day. So much had happened over the past year: Matt had received his master's degree, Zack and Tommy had been adopted on Valentine's Day, and now Liza and Luis were becoming a permanent part of our family. How had we gotten to this point? We had never planned on adopting six kids, yet there we were, back in Houston, with two teenagers ready to take our name.

Around six and a half years before their adoption day, I had stood as still as a deer in a meadow, gazing into the little brown eyes of our four-week-old son Alex. At that moment, I would have never imagined that after our first paper pregnancy, we would eventually "birth" five more children through the same process, that I would stand again, and again, and again, and again, and again, gazing into brown eyes, two pairs of them being the eyes of teenagers.

Back in the beginning, when we had first started pursuing adoption, my heart had been reeling from the grief and loneliness of infertility and my vision had been tunneled toward a baby: that baby I could never birth. I had needed and craved for our first adoption to be of an infant. My heart had been shattered from the loss of the possibility of pregnancy. Even years later with six children in our home, I grieved the lost opportunity of carrying a biological child, of never experiencing childbirth, of never looking into the eyes of someone created in the bonds of my marriage to Matt and who was physically a part of us. Adoption hadn't doused that desire, even though adoption had been our first choice to create our family after we had learned of our infertility.

Only when I truly grieved the loss of pregnancy did I move on to the blessed gift of acceptance. My children were my children, just as if I had birthed them, but it was okay to grieve the loss of pregnancy. It was also okay to let go and move on— that's what acceptance allows you to do.

After Alex, our baby, had come Carlosse, a toddler, and my heart had begun to stretch. As these two children had grafted into our family and as we fostered kids of all different ages before moving to Texas, I began to see that as I allowed my heart to expand, so did my opportunities to love.

Six years after our first infant adoption, and after our toddler adoptions, we journeyed into the too-little-trodden path of older-child adoption. Really, we happened upon it. Were we planning on teenagers in our home? Well, yes, eventually after the boys had grown, but most certainly not as adoptive placements. No, it hadn't been on our radar at all, but through the tiny brown hands of a little boy named Zack had come not one but two older children.

The decision to say yes on the phone call for Liza and Luis began our journey into the world of teenagers…and not just any teenagers. These teenagers had been in thirteen schools and countless homes, apartments, and shelters. For two years, they had been in foster care in a home that spoke only Spanish, causing them through immersion to learn the language. Now, on Adoption Day, they were adjusting to a new mom and dad, brothers, and a new city right in the middle of junior high and high school.

Have we ever really stopped to place ourselves in the shoes of the numerous children in foster care? So many teens sit in foster care, waiting for homes, but really, they are waiting to age-out because there are no homes for them. In fact, more than 23,000 foster children every year are emancipated from the system. They are the hard to place, the kids nobody wants, or just the kids people are too terrified to consider. They are kids like Liza and Luis.

But we had considered. We had thought long and hard about what would happen to Liza and Luis if we said no. We had fast-forwarded in our minds to the likelihood that they would not leave foster care and would not find a forever family. We had known that they may even be separated if they were moved from their current foster home. We had known that the odds of finding an adoptive home for both to stay together were stacked against them. We had thought about how we had the power to offer hope, the ability to bring back together a family that had been shattered into fragments that had landed all over the state of Texas. We had thought about their futures and about how we could lead them, guide them, encourage them, and love them. We had known that we could, so we did.

On January 9, 2009, exactly five years after we had brought Carlosse home, we would be bringing our teenage "babies" home. They had adjusted somewhat to our home in Dallas and started over for the last time at their new schools. Liza was a freshman and Luis a sixth grader. This was our fourth time going to court for adoption. Because we hadn't known any better, we had finalized Alex's adoption over the phone on October 31, 2003. Another foster mom had strongly suggested that, for convenience, we just adopt over the phone, and in our naivety, that's what we had done. Later, we wished we had driven up to Spokane and gone to court. If you can go to court to adopt, go. Going to court is a joyful and profound experience, especially if family can join you.

For our next adoption, with Carlosse, we had traveled to Spokane on August 19, 2004, for finalization. I will never forget the words the judge spoke over us that day with Matt's family present: "By the power vested in me by the State of Washington, I declare Carlosse to be your son, just as if you bore him."

I had physically felt the change of possession after the judge declared Carlosse a Tschirgi. It was a shifting. He was really and truly ours. His birth certificate had our names on it, like we had been at the hospital and I had given birth.

Zack and Tommy had been adopted together on February 14, 2009. My mom had flown to Texas for their adoption. We had gotten rooms at a hotel downtown and had stayed thirty floors up. Liza and Luis had pressed their faces against the window and marveled at the scene down below. Aside from their one time in an airplane, that was the highest up they had ever been.

Six months later, we traveled down to Houston one more time, to officially add Liza and Luis to the Tschirgi family. What would this adoption be like?

Arriving at the court house was different this time, because the kids we were adopting truly knew what was happening. They had been part of the decision process. They had said yes to us, not just us to them. This time, adoption felt like a marriage ceremony. It was a holy moment, the joining of our families. We were the bridegroom, and Liza and Luis were the bride. They took our name, and we chose each other. We promised to love them and treat them just as if we had borne them. They had chosen us to be their new mom and dad. We made a commitment—a commitment that would be tested by the trials of life, past abuse, neglect, and abandonment, but a commitment that would hold strong through even the most difficult of times. God had joined us. Hard times were not going to separate us. For better or worse, for sickness and in health, we were mom and dad, and they were our kids. Forever.

So, on that hot, humid day down in a Houston, Texas, courthouse, the judge declared us legally a family. We knew, however, that we already were a family: a family built through adoption. A family born out of some of the most difficult trials yet founded on some of the greatest love. We were a childless couple who were childless no more, and six motherless and fatherless kids who were motherless and fatherless no more.

Looking back, today, I can see every stretch mark I have borne on my heart. Looking behind, I know how those stretch marks got there. Looking ahead, I know I will see more stretch marks on my heart.

Afterword

A Call to Action

This book is a love story. Several love stories. Stories about how broken hearts, against all odds, found one another in a hurting world and became something new and strong and beautiful. You may feel a tug at your heartstrings right now. You may wonder, "How can I be a part of bringing newness and healing and beauty into the life of a child without a family?"

My husband and I felt a similar tug at our heartstrings when we bought our first house. It was a little farmhouse with three bedrooms and one bath. We were a young couple with one daughter. She was in one room, we were in another, and the third bedroom held boxes I didn't feel like unpacking. Until one day I carried out the last few boxes and the room was empty. I remember standing in the doorway, mulling our options for this freed-up space. A craft room? Workout space? A home office? Then, truly, I had a clear vision this was a space we should give away. A room we should share. Specifically, with children. We started foster parent training the next month and added a foster son to our family just six months later.

There is a huge need for foster parents in every corner of our nation. Children of all ages need a safe place to land after enduring abuse, neglect, and removal from their families. My husband and I went on to foster for ten more years. Our biological children have grown up with a revolving door of brothers and sisters who come for a time, then move back or move on. And a few who are ours forever. It's made our kids strong and kind and generous and tough. Foster parenting as a family has taught our kids things I could never have modeled or instilled. Compassion is deep-seated and free-flowing in our family. We've seen God work miracles right under our roof.

You may not be sure you're in the "right place" to begin fostering or to add to your family through adoption. And while that may be true, many families who are capable find themselves tripped up or stalled out due to fear or misinformation. Here are some of the most common things we hear from people who choose to delay or decide against fostering or adopting:

My kids are still little.

My kids are almost out of the house.

I can have kids of my own.

We're too young.

I'm too old.

Our house is small.

We live in an apartment.

I'm single.

I work full time.

Our budget is already very tight.

We don't want to adopt.

We only want to adopt.

We could never love a child and let them go.

We could never love a child that is not our own.

I've walked alongside many families who felt, initially, that these concerns disqualified or prevented them from fostering or even adopting. I would challenge you to talk through these issues with someone who has fostered or adopted. Or have a chat with a child-placing agency about your options and requirements. But mostly, I would reflect on the root of these concerns. Is there an underlying fear you need to work through, or are there legitimate reasons you should not open your home?

And fostering isn't for everyone.

That's right. If you read a book like this and don't feel called to open your home to a child in need, that is A-OK.

But you're not off the hook.

There are many other ways you can (and should) have an impact on the lives of children in foster care. Foster children need mentors and advocates. Foster and adoptive families need childcare, support, hand-me-downs, casserole deliveries, and encouragement. If you're not called to foster or adopt, find ways to rally around those who are.

As foster parents, we were so grateful when someone would reach out and ask how they could help our family care for kids. Sometimes I brushed off these offers, but my sweet, persistent friends and family learned to impose a little help on me. They would walk up, calendar in hand, and say, "When can I give you two a date night?" I have literally pulled up to my house after a long day of work and errands and appointments for kids to find a piping-hot lasagna and sides dishes just sitting on my front porch. A little garlic bread after a day in the trenches can really help a gal go the distance. I signed foster children up for soccer, then checked our account to find their fees had been paid by someone from our church. Retired teachers came by after school to tutor. A friend from work dropped by to teach me how to care for a child whose hair texture was very different from my own. Men from our neighborhood pitched in to assemble our swing set. Some of them don't even *like* children, and yet they found a way to help. The list goes on and on.

And each one of these small gestures was an investment not only in our kids but in the stability and health of our family. Literally, a load off my husband and myself. By supporting our family, these people were helping sustain us through the ups and downs of fostering.

If you don't personally know someone who is a foster or adoptive parent, you may start looking for a nonprofit to volunteer with. In many areas, CASA (Court Appointed Special Advocates) volunteers go through specialized training to become the child's voice in the court system. Being a CASA requires no legal or specialized background, as all the training is provided. It's a big commitment, but CASA efforts have a considerable effect on the outcomes of the children they serve. For more information, visit www.CASAforChildren.org. Also, local churches across the nation are beginning to awaken to the unique needs of children in foster care and their caregivers in their own backyards. If you would like to start a ministry at your church or learn about practical ways your church body can serve families in your community, look into equipping ministries such as Embrace at www.Embrace-Texas.org (not just for Texans) or Christian Alliance for Orphans (CAFO) at www.CAFO.org. If you live in an area where few resources exist, consider that your eyes may have been opened to this need so you could be the one to initiate services for children and families.

You.

Right where you are.

In the place you are planted.

You can make a difference. Find your niche! Use your talents and interests and gifts for good, and change some little lives in the process.

Denise Kendrick
Executive Director
Embrace Texas

Notes

Infertility Statistics

www.mayoclinic.org/diseases-conditions/male-infertility/basics/.../con-20033113

https://www.asrm.org/detail.aspx?id=2322

Foster Care Statistics

https://www.acf.hhs.gov/cb/research-data-technology/statistics-research/afcars

https://www.fosterclub.com/article/statistics-foster-care

https://www.nfyi.org/51-useful-aging-out-of-foster-care-statistics-social-race-media/

Starfish Story

http://www.eiseley.org/Star_Thrower_Cook.pdf

University of Texas at Houston Statistics

http://www.tmc.edu/about-tmc/facts-and-figures/

About the Author:
Niki Breeser Tschirgi

Niki Breeser Tschirgi is a stay-at-home mom who resides in Spokane, Washington, with her husband, Matt; six adopted children (four boys still at home, ages eleven through sixteen); and Moose, her standard poodle. She discovered her love for writing in the seventh grade and studied creative writing at the University of Idaho. Niki wrote for *Blindigo* online magazine while living in Houston, Texas, and over the years has published several blogs, including "The Stars Are Bright—How a Northern Girl Became a Southern Woman and Everything In-Between" and "Rock a Child's World," a blog that raised awareness for adoption in Texas. Niki's first book, *Growing up Alaska* is a memoir about her crazy, freezing childhood in the interior of Alaska. Niki's second book, *Stretch-mark My Heart*, shares her family's adoption journey through the US foster care system.

When she isn't writing, doing laundry, loading dishes, or sweeping the floor, Niki can be found reading, practicing yoga, or paddleboarding with her kids. To connect with Niki, follow her on Facebook (www.facebook.com/niki.tschirgi) or Twitter (@nikitschirgi).

CPSIA information can be obtained
at www.ICGtesting.com
Printed in the USA
LVOW05*0250160218
566779LV00001B/2/P

9 781457 562150